T0110569

From Here
to Where???

Gabriel Silva Lamboglia

BALBOA.
PRESS
A DIVISION OF HAY HOUSE

Balboa Press books may be ordered through booksellers or by contacting:

Balboa Press
A Division of Hay House
1663 Liberty Drive
Bloomington, IN 47403
www.balboapress.com
1 (877) 407-4847

Because of the dynamic nature of the Internet, any web addresses or links contained in this book may have changed since publication and may no longer be valid. The views expressed in this work are solely those of the author and do not necessarily reflect the views of the publisher, and the publisher hereby disclaims any responsibility for them.

The author of this book does not dispense medical advice or prescribe the use of any technique as a form of treatment for physical, emotional, or medical problems without the advice of a physician, either directly or indirectly. The intent of the author is only to offer information of a general nature to help you in your quest for emotional and spiritual well-being. In the event you use any of the information in this book for yourself, which is your constitutional right, the author and the publisher assume no responsibility for your actions.

Any people depicted in stock imagery provided by Thinkstock are models, and such images are being used for illustrative purposes only.
Certain stock imagery © Thinkstock.

Printed in the United States of America.

ISBN: 978-1-4525-8777-6 (sc)
ISBN: 978-1-4525-8778-3 (hc)
ISBN: 978-1-4525-8776-9 (e)

Library of Congress Control Number: 2013921890

Balboa Press rev. date: 05/12/2014

Contents

Special Thanks

It takes a village to write a book. I want to thank all these people because they put their own lives aside to help me put this book together.

My daughter, Sophia, spent hours, days and months translating from Spanish to English then sending the copy back and forth to me for editing. Her dedication to the success of my project gives me great pride and makes me feel really special. As a father, I feel I have earned her respect because she went through this painful process with me. I know I always can count on her. For these reasons, and so many more, I would have never been able to make this project possible without her help.

To my son, Fernando, the most patient son a man could have. His unconditional love, heartfelt honesty, and appreciation of nature teach me to be a better person every day. While writing this book, he was always there to show me how everything is in perfect harmony. The time and dedication he put into helping me with the cover design is priceless. His help in what may seem small ways to him will always mean a great deal to me.

I will be forever grateful to my parents who gave me their unconditional love and taught me through their example to never stop trying.

To my friend, Fred Ponzlov, who has read this book several times as he helped me and guided me through every step of the process. It's a big compliment to have someone travelling on business to Prague and he writes an email that says he is thinking about the book. I simply do not have enough words to thank him.

To April, who questioned her sanity at the beginning about taking this project but says she accepted because of my sincerity and generosity of spirit. Once we started working, she has done more than I ever expected to assist me in making this project come true.

To Tom Kelly, who somehow understood my concepts and ideas spot-on the first time. His illustrations clearly say everything I want to show. Without his help, I never would have had the full vision of my book realized.

To Melissa, who spent hours with me working on the interpretation of my thoughts sometimes until three or four in the morning. I am grateful for her dedication, her unlimited time and for believing in my project. She put her own work second to help me with mine. For this, I extend my deepest gratitude.

I must thank everyone on my team. These are the people who keep everything going and under control. Every day I know our customers are happy and the business is running. Their incredible hard work and dedication to the success of our business, gave me free time to complete this project.

To my wife, Laura, without her patience and support I don't know where I would be today nor would I have the great family I am so proud to be part of. She stands beside me in every endeavor, understands me and puts up with me, which is not easy!

I love you with all my heart.

Foreword

How does someone make the journey from being a chicken farmer in Uruguay to becoming a success in the United States? Someone who arrived with a thick accent and no understanding of the English language? This is the intriguing question I posed to myself when I first met Gabriel Silva Lamboglia in the early 1990s. Not that he offered this information to me, I discovered he is too humble to offer his success story on a first, second or even fifteenth meeting. But I slowly came to realize the extent of his business acumen over the weeks that he spent with me in my acting class. I also began to understand his unique views of both the business world and the world we live in.

I know there are many Horatio Alger stories in America, but none that I ever witnessed firsthand. Gabriel has become successful in a way only MBA graduates can only dream of. Yet, this will not be one of your usual how-to, "I can be a millionaire" books. You won't find these concepts in any MBA course at Wharton. This is a methodology unique to Gabriel and his common sense approach to business: A man who found his own way, through experience and through trial and error.

Told through some well-known and some not so well-known maxims that have guided his way, Gabriel shows the reader how he directly applied a positive and take action attitude to any situation on hand. This wisdom infuses his decision-making process and helps him overcome countless obstacles that stood in his way toward success. Gabriel is a common man who found his way through the business mine field and along the way managed to hold onto his intense humanity and love of his fellow man.

Gabriel now presents these concepts to you in his own, very personal manner through anecdotes that illustrate his maxim-driven philosophy. The ideas that he presents in this book will make sense to you. They made sense to me because they were common sense. I know there will be items that will resonate in a way that will make you think and discover your own path to success, your own victorious journey.

Truly inspirational, this is the story of one amazing self-made man.

—Fred Ponzlov
Screenwriter and Theatre Director and co-author of "Solomon Speaks on Reconnecting Your Life"

Introduction

If you think running your own business is as difficult as trying to roll a square tire, it's not, and I can show you an easy way of doing it.

Money, well-managed, provides security. Security, well-managed, provides independence. Independence, well-managed, provides freedom. Freedom, well-managed, provides happiness.

1: Happiness is not something ready-made. It comes from your own actions. – Dalai Lama

How to achieve this goal and how to read this book

This book can be read in two ways. Those of you who are impatient, like me, can skip directly to the list of proverbs and sayings in the back of the book that have guided me in my life. For those of you who are patient and like details, I recommend you read the entire book.

I believe sayings, proverbs, and maxims enhance our lives and are mechanisms for learning from the past and passing on wisdom to future generations. I do not remember where I first heard the sayings I live by or exactly how they became a part of my life. Some of the sayings grew out of personal observations and experiences. I do want to make it clear that I adopted the majority of the sayings from other people.

Throughout this book, I explain how I applied or modified these sayings in real situations to guide me on my path in times of uncertainty.

The way you choose to apply the sayings and information in this book will determine the results you achieve. However you choose to read the book, I hope you will embrace these sayings and incorporate them into your daily life to help you through uncertain times and to achieve the happiness you desire.

—Gabriel Silva Lamboglia

Chapter 1

Telling our story

I have learned that everybody wants to live at the top of the mountain without realizing that true happiness lies in the way we climb the slope.
—Johnny Welch (often attributed to Gabriel Garcia Marquez)

People always ask me to tell them the story of how my wife, Laura, and I came to live in the United States. I don't know if it is because people find our lives interesting, or if it is because the way I tell the story is funny. What I do know is that people like stories. One of the questions I am repeatedly asked is what our life was like in Uruguay before we moved to the United State, how we adapted, and what we sacrificed in pursuit of the American dream.

For years I kept telling myself that one day I would put it all down on paper, but I never did, until now. Today, while I was looking at a book of political cartoons by the Argentine cartoonist Joaquin Salvador Lavado, better known as 'Quino', I found a reason to tell my story.

2: A picture is worth a thousand words.

Quino's book, "Fine, thank you. And you?" is a collection of cartoons reflecting South America's socioeconomic situation in the 1970's. Ironically, and what inspired me to tell my story, Quino's book reflected the current socioeconomic situation in the United States and throughout the world. I marvelled that a social situation drawn forty years ago still applies today. If the publication date were changed, no one would know it was from the 1970's!

In fact, Quino's book applied to numerous periods throughout history. I was shocked to discover how true it was that "history repeats itself" and even more disheartened by the fact that the reason history repeats itself is because people make the same mistakes time and again.

Throughout time human beings keep tripping over the same stone.

I considered the role I played in the scheme of life. I could not stop history from repeating itself. I could tell others how I weathered the storm in the bad times and made the most of the good times. The best way for me to do this was to tell my story and describe the methods I used to survive the bad times and enjoy the good.

I am still surprised by how Laura and I got where we are today. The only way I can explain it is through the poem *"Walker"* by Antonio Machado:

> Traveler, your footsteps make the path,
> and nothing more.
>
> Traveler, there is no path,
> the path is made by travelling.
>
> Travelling you make the road,
> and looking back
> you see the path you will never trod again.
>
> Traveler, there is no path,
> only wakes upon the sea.

Translated by Sophia Silva

In Uruguay, I raised hens and sold their eggs. When I think about going from being a chicken farmer to living the American Dream, I realize in life you must be flexible, recognize opportunities, and not be afraid to try new things and work hard. When people say I am lucky, I tell them the truth: the more I work and the more I expose myself to new opportunities, the luckier I get.

3: Strike while the iron is hot.

Work is a form of entertainment for me, a hobby. I do not count hours or measure the amount of effort I put in to work. I never focus on what the result of my efforts will be. I concentrate on the now, seize the moment and strive to be the best I can. I never let time go to waste because time is a treasure we cannot buy and the present is a gift to enjoy now.

My work is done once I am proud of the result. Until then, I know there is more work to be done. Like artists and writers who work until they are satisfied without knowing if anyone will buy their artwork or book, when I do something, I do it to the best of my ability without consideration of financial reward or personal recognition.

A STORY: Jack desperately wanted everyone to see him as highly intelligent. He dedicated all of his efforts to reach this goal, but he could never achieve it. One day he decided to stop trying to impress people and instead concentrate on just doing his best. From that day, people commented how smart Jack was.

4: Quality is pride of workmanship.

Chapter 2

Why the USA

To get where we are today, Laura and I sacrificed greatly and remained open-minded in our search for opportunities. I am where I am today because of her support. She supported me in every endeavor, understood me and put up with me, which is not easy!

When we decided to come to the United States, she was six months pregnant and neither of us spoke English. We left Uruguay on a cold afternoon in May. Actually, I am not sure whether it was actually cold, or if my fears and uncertainties made me feel cold. On the day of our departure, friends and family surrounded us at the airport. On the surface, I acted confident to convince everyone we had made the right decision and to show I had everything under control. Despite my bravado, I was very scared. I avoided direct eye contact with my friends and family because I was afraid if they looked into my eyes they would see my doubts and fears.

I remember the look of desolation on my in-laws' faces. They were inconsolable as their only daughter was moving far away, to a foreign country with an unfamiliar language. As we waited for our flight to be called, the tension in the air was so thick you could cut it with a knife. I knew many people were thinking the same things:

- Why leave? You can be successful here.
- Who will help you when you need something? Laura is pregnant.
- Where will you live? This is your country. Your family is here. You are crazy.

The only person courageous enough to ask these questions was Eduardo, Laura's father, and he kept repeating them. A part of all of us wished time would stand still and they would not call us to board the airplane.

The agony became so maddening we decided to say our final goodbyes and go through to the passenger-only area, the point of no return. Certain we were making the right decision but sad to leave family and friends, both Laura and I cried as we boarded the plane. As we took off for our new life, I forced myself to stop worrying about the many uncertainties. It was best to wait until we got there.

5: I will see how deep the river is once I start to cross it.

We moved to the United States because the deteriorating economic conditions in Uruguay made chicken farming no longer viable. Continuing to farm would have meant failure and economic disaster. I had to do something to earn a living and repay our debts. The question was, "What?" I began searching for a way out. Around this same time, I attended a Chamber of Commerce meeting and by chance met an industrialist in the natural stone trade. Curious by nature about how things are made, I asked to visit his operation. He agreed and promised to have his manager arrange a time.

At this point, I should tell you I am dyslexic and often see things differently than most people. The day I visited the factory, it seemed obvious to me that a few minor adjustments to the production order would significantly increase productivity. I casually mentioned this to the manager and thought nothing else about it.

After the tour, I went to the office to thank the owner for arranging the tour. In the course of our conversation, he told me he wanted to expand his market and start a marble and granite distribution company in the United States but had not finalized the details of the business plan. Although I knew nothing about the stone business, I listened with interest, never imagining he would consider hiring me.

Two weeks later the owner called and asked to meet with me. We met and he explained more about his plans for starting up in the United States and said they wanted me to head up the operation in America and, if possible, start immediately. Shocked by his unexpected offer, I asked him to please repeat what he had said. He repeated his offer and told me to consider it and get back to him.

That night, while Laura prepared dinner, I replayed the meeting. At first she did not take me seriously and suggested I misunderstood, or the company was making empty promises. Both skeptical, we decided to wait a few days to see what happened.

In my mind the question kept popping up, "Why would they choose me?" I didn't speak English. I didn't have experience with natural stone. I did not have knowledge of the American market.

6: You can't get something for nothing. If it sounds too good to be true, it probably is not good at all.

Two days later the owner phoned and asked if I had made a decision. I told him I had not but would like to learn more about the job description and the compensation.

As it turned out, they were serious and offered me a base salary plus twelve thousand dollars for housing and furniture. They also agreed to pay for our trip, Laura's medical bills and English classes for both of us.

The job offer in place, Laura and I analyzed our business loans to determine how much we owed and then calculated our repayments based on my earnings. If we were frugal and managed our money carefully, we could repay our debt in a little over a year. Once we repaid our debt, we could begin to think about our next step.

I realized how fortunate I was to have a second chance to apply everything I had learned. I could not have asked for more, and I hoped to be wise enough not to repeat the same mistakes again.

7: He who has nothing to lose has everything to gain.

Chapter 3

When I was a child

I grew up in an upper-middle-class family. My mother was a dentist and my father a physical trainer in the military. Most families owned one car, mine owned two or three. In Uruguay, in the 1970's, the number of cars you owned defined your social class. My family traveled each year and owned a vacation home in the countryside.

I have had a spirit of independence all my life. The summer I turned nine I decided I wanted my own money and needed a job. I approached my parents with my idea and promised to maintain my grades if they allowed me to get a job. Lifelong learners, my parents made education a priority. My mother often read and studied to keep abreast of the latest dental technologies and methods, and my father studied to climb the ranks. To gain my parents' consent, I knew education had to be part of my proposition.

8: The secret to receiving the desired answer is in formulating the right question.

A STORY: Two young monks, who loved to smoke, wondered if they were allowed to smoke while praying. After discussing the subject for several days, they could not reach a conclusion so they decided to ask their respective superiors for advice.

The next time they met, the first monk quickly asked, "What did your abbot tell you? Can you smoke?"

The second monk shook his head, "No, he was furious and chastised me for asking! What about you? What did your abbot say?"

The first monk shrugged, "My abbot was very pleased with me. He said it was not a problem." Then he thought for a moment and said, "What exactly did you ask?"

"I asked if I could smoke while I prayed," said the second monk.

"Ah," the first monk said wisely, "That's the problem. I asked if I could pray while I smoked."

My parents accepted my proposal. I suspect they thought no one would hire a nine year old and if they did, it would not last long.

This marked the beginning of my journey for financial independence, which continues today; a journey peppered with wins and losses, with every successful endeavor accompanied by a few mistakes.

I have always been and still am fascinated with acting and cinematography. The idea of imparting emotions and conveying positive and motivational messages through storytelling intrigues me. My ideal job would have been something in the film industry. Unfortunately, Uruguay did not have a film industry at the time, so I set out to discover what jobs were available.

I started with the local pizza bar. Each day after school, I showed up at the bar and volunteered to help with anything they needed. At first they ignored me and did not take me seriously, but I persisted and continued to show up every day.

9: Let your work speak to your character even when you're not around.

After a few days, they gave me small tasks to complete. I gladly did whatever was asked of me. After a couple of weeks, they began leaving the dirty cups and plates in the sink for me to wash. I realized they relied on my help. In Uruguay in the 1970's, automatic dishwashers were not commonplace. I washed everything by hand. At first it took hours, but I quickly learned to be more efficient and faster. When I completed one task, I asked for another. This attitude won the respect of my boss and my co-workers.

Seeing my eagerness to learn and the quality of my work, the pizzamaker offered to teach me to make pizzas. I eagerly accepted this offer on the spot.

The server pulled me aside when he heard this and reminded me that my earnings came entirely from tips from the servers. If I wanted to continue receiving these tips, in addition to washing dishes, I would now have to help clean the bathrooms. Without hesitation, I assured him this was no problem.

I now had three jobs and was not even on the payroll! Throughout my life, my work ethic of being reliable, taking initiative and being willing to learn new skills has led to many opportunities. I have the same attitude today as I did when I was nine.

My true day of triumph came the day the owner, Perfecto, asked me to run the cash register. This was an honor! No one other than Perfecto touched the cash register, which was positioned in the middle of the service counter where you could see everything happening in the restaurant. Because I was too short to operate the register, I had to sit on high bar stool.

This was one of the proudest days of my life. I had only hoped for a small job, and now the owner trusted me enough to ask me to do something he allowed no one else to do. I worked at the pizza bar for approximately four months and earned decent pay for my age. I knew, however, this was not the life I wanted. It was time to move on.

One final note on the pizza bar: Perfecto was a Spanish immigrant, 100% dedicated to his work. He lived behind the bar and was the first person to arrive each morning and the last to leave each night. Eight years after I left the pizza bar, I heard Perfecto had opened two new restaurants, one in the most expensive part of the city. I gained a renewed appreciation for his work ethic and, proud to have worked for him, I went to visit him at his new restaurant. I saw him behind the cash register. With the exception of his gray hair and a few wrinkles, Perfecto had not changed. I had changed considerably and grown from a child into a teenager. At first, Perfecto did not recognize me but as soon as I said my name, he became very emotional and invited me to stay and order whatever I wanted.

He sat with me and told me how he had come from Spain and started his pizza business. I told him about my life. As I left, Perfecto assured me there would always be a job for me in his restaurants. That was the last time I spoke to him. But I am getting ahead of myself.

10: Persevere and you will triumph.

Chapter 4

Looking for opportunities

When I was ten, I left the pizza bar in search of a new job. Each day on my way home from school, I walked past a local body shop. The guys were always moving the cars around by having one person behind the wheel and the others pushing. It occurred to me that if I worked there, maybe I could be the person behind the wheel. I could learn to drive and earn money!

> *For everyone who asks, receives. Everyone who seeks, finds.*
> *And to everyone who knocks, the door will be opened.*
> —*Matthew 7:8, New Living Translation*

The next day, I went in and spoke with the owner. I explained that I lived in the neighborhood and would like to help out in the afternoons after school to learn about cars. He agreed on the condition I avoided any hazardous work. Unlike the pizza place, the body shop was full of equipment, heavy materials, and a variety of young immature guys who loved playing practical jokes.

The owner assigned one of the best employees the task of restoring a collectible car to its original condition. Over the course of a few days, this guy worked painstakingly, priming the car and trying different colors until he found the perfect match. Just before he started painting, he set the paint gun down and went to the restroom. As a joke, one of the other guys switched the paint in the gun. Everyone laughed hysterically, except for the guy working on the car, and me. I saw the devastation on his face and felt so sorry for him that it made it impossible for me to laugh.

Another practical joke was hiding clothes. Working in the shop was dirty and sweaty business. Before going home, the employees always showered and the last person usually came out to find his clothes missing.

Being the smallest and lightest employee, I was the ideal person to steer the cars while the other guys pushed them to a new location. One day I decided to play a trick of my own. I put my foot on the brake and laughed as I watched in the rearview mirror as the others struggled to push the car.

I admired the owner of the shop who handed me my money every payday. I saved until I had enough to buy an old motorcycle. I could hardly wait to start taking the engine apart and putting it back together. The day I brought it home, I parked it in the middle of the driveway so everyone could see it.

When my mother came home, instead of hello, she said, "Whose motorcycle is in the drive?" I proudly answered, "Mine." I knew I was in for trouble when she said, "We'll talk about this when your father gets home."

As soon as my father walked in, my mother called him into the kitchen and closed the door. Minutes later my father emerged and, like an army general, commanded, "Return it." I did not dare disobey his orders, so I said, "Yes sir," and returned the motorcycle to the shop. I explained my problem to the owner. After listening attentively, he said he would take the motorcycle back but he would not return my money.

Unwilling to lose my hard earned money, I returned home with the motorcycle hoping that when my parents heard I would be losing my money if I returned the bike, they might change their mind and allow me to keep it. Before I finished explaining the situation, my father interrupted and said, "no one gave you permission to buy it," so I had to return it.

I returned to the shop hoping the owner might agree to sell the motorcycle for me and return some of my money. Unfortunately, he was not as compassionate of a man as I had imagined. Having no other option, I gave him the motorcycle and walked home with no motorcycle and no money.

That day I learned there would forever be someone above me who had the last word.

11: Where a captain rules, a sailor has no sway.

Chapter 5

Keep searching

I decided to change jobs when two of my friends told me how much money they were making as altar boys at our neighborhood church. In return for helping the priest with mass, we were allowed to work at the weddings where we earned large tips from the grooms' fathers and godfathers. If they forgot to tip us, we politely reminded them in front of their friends. This worked well because the gentlemen, not wanting to be seen denying young altar boys their tip, were usually quite generous.

One day the church vacuum broke so I offered to take it to the local repair shop. While speaking with the owner of the shop, a man named Eduardo, a new idea occurred to me. If I could find more appliances that needed repair, perhaps Eduardo would give me commission for every appliance I brought to him. Eduardo liked the idea. The deal benefited both us: Eduardo's business increased and I made money without investing any capital.

I started going around to all the houses in my neighborhood, asking if they had any appliances that needed to be fixed and offering them a free estimate. Since everyone knew and trusted me, they gave me their appliances. I took the appliances to Eduardo who told me the charges to fix the pieces. I then reported these rates back to my neighbors.

After I started bringing in a lot of business, I asked Eduardo to give me better prices for the appliances. I eventually brought him so much business he couldn't complete the orders on time. That was when I asked him if I could work with him.

I learned a lot about repairs while I worked there. I learned how to repair televisions, radios, vacuums, coffee makers, and various other appliances. Business was good until the import laws changed, making the price of new appliances so cheap it was no longer economical to have them repaired. Everyone wanted new products and seemingly overnight the appliance repair shop went out of business.

I was now around thirteen and had worked at the pizza bar, the body shop, the church, and the appliance repair shop. In order to devote more time to studying, I gave up my job and in my free time helped my mom at her dental office and learned to develop the X-rays.

One day I came across an advertisement in a dental magazine for a red acrylic box that developed X-rays without the need for a black room. Fascinated by the concept, I decided to fabricate the boxes myself and sell them to all the dentists I knew. I thought this would be a perfect opportunity for me to start a business.

The next day I started production. For the boxes, I bought sheets of red acrylic at a place that made street signs. On the front of the box, I cut two round holes and inserted rubber rings, purchased from an auto supply shop. I attached sweater sleeves to the rings to allow the developer to reach in but keep the light out. That's how I made my first three X-ray developing boxes.

After testing the boxes, I set out to sell them to local dentists. When I pointed out the convenience of developing X-rays without leaving the room, the boxes sold quickly. The boxes were cheap, easy to make, and easy to sell. Deciding there was a good outlook for this business. I invested all of my money in materials and built as many developing boxes as possible, fully expecting them to sell.

Unfortunately, some predictions aren't always correct. The first boxes sold easily and at a good price, the second round took longer to sell, and the third round was almost impossible to sell. I was left with a room full of X-ray developing boxes without a clue what to do with them.

Fortunately, I made a deal with one of the dentists to buy all of the boxes and was able to recoup most of my investment.

12: Don't bite off more than you can chew.

Chapter 6

My teenage years

The years went by, I got older, the economy got better, and the construction industry boomed. I have learned throughout the years that construction is the first industry to grow when the economy is doing well, and the first industry to suffer when the economy is bad. Since the construction industry relies on other industries for supplies, I decided to take advantage of the boom and get into the plywood industry.

A company called Samic Rio de la Plata manufactured plywood from eucalyptus trees. I decided to start a business supplying Samic with eucalyptus trunks. I located a tract of land dense in eucalyptus trees and negotiated a price with the owner allowing me to harvest trees of a certain diameter. I planned to use one hundred percent of the product by cutting the trees to Samic's requirements and selling the offcuts as firewood.

I was not old enough to have a driver's license, so I subcontracted the delivery of the wood to a neighbor who owned a sizeable truck which they used twice a week to transport produce. This solved the problem of delivering the eucalyptus trunks to Samic.

I was in a new league and no longer the little kid on the block whom everyone knew. My responsibilities were much greater and my business required capital to purchase tools, pay for transportation, cover the cost of repairs, and employ someone to help me. I used my savings to cover these expenses until I received my first payment from Samic.

The business thrived until the economy fell and along with it the construction industry, which reduced the demand for eucalyptus wood. With no demand for my product, I closed the business. On the positive side, the business required minimal investment, we did not have an office, a workshop or a retail outlet, and I subcontracted the truck. I simply walked away with my chainsaw, tools, and a considerable amount of capital.

I began to look for the next opportunity. I read in the newspaper about a new law allowing the tax-free importation of cars for racing purposes. A car used in races for two years could also be sold tax-free. In Uruguay, the tax on imported vehicles was exorbitant. This seemed like an excellent opportunity to make a profit doing something I dreamed of doing: racing cars. I would purchase a car for racing purposes at a reduced, tax-free amount, race for two years and be able to sell the car for a profit.

I found a car in Brazil and my cousin Beatriz went with me to pick up and bring the car to Uruguay. To race, I needed a sponsor. Fortunately, Pedro Cabarcos, the owner of a racing team took me on. We both loved modifying cars' engines and often stayed up all night working on our cars to improve their performance.

I loved racing and I was good at it. Then I had a serious accident. The accident was on the front page of every newspaper. Although the accident scared me badly, I continued racing until my two-year contract expired and then I sold the car and retired from racing having made money pursuing a hobby and getting the need to race out of my system.

13: Water under the bridge.

I wanted to find a steady occupation but I didn't know what I wanted to do. Plus I was still in school at the time. Although I found school difficult and was not a particularly good student, my parents insisted I continue studying and make my education a priority.

I continued my education and my search for the ideal job. I liked the idea of flying airplanes so I began researching pilot training programs and their prerequisites. Aviation in Uruguay was limited to our Air Force. To be considered for the pilot program required serving two years before they decided if you qualified or if you would be what they called, "navigator of various roles." Few people were selected to become pilots because the military possessed minimal airplanes.

Joining the military was out of the question for me, so I wrote to commercial airlines abroad and inquired about available positions in their training programs and their requirements for admittance. In the midst of all this, a medical examination revealed I was color-blind to red and green. The news devastated me; one of the major requirements for aviation was not being color-blind.

The test for color-blindness consists of a series of numbers embedded in colored circles. Individuals with normal eyesight can see the numbers. Individuals who are color-blind cannot see the numbers, regardless of angle, lighting or distance. Desperate to pass the color-blind test, I made several attempts but had to admit I could not see the numbers.

14: Every cloud has a silver lining.

Discovering my color-blindness explained why I had struggled in certain areas. For example, in high school, my teacher held up my drawing of a tree as an example of something unique and then proceeded to say it was an example of a high school student who had not learned their colors. To my dismay, I had used a red marker for the trunk because to my eyes, red looked brown. I was humiliated and wanted to hide! After that, I devised a system. Whenever we used markers for a project, I observed the students next to me. As soon as one finished with a marker I asked to use it before it was returned to the box with the other markers.

A man's errors are his portals of discovery. – James Joyce

Over the next three years, I continued my search for the right profession. I studied oceanography, and when that did not suit me I joined the Navy to become an officer; that did not suit me so I switched to systems engineering. None of these studies fulfilled me, yet I knew I could not continue changing majors on a whim.

Society places immense pressure on young people to choose a university career at a very young age. I felt this and suspected people viewed me as a failure for starting and not following through. I never viewed myself as a failure. I knew it was a matter of not finding the right profession for me. I also knew I would continue the search until I found a career that satisfied and fulfilled me.

This was a crossroads in my life and I did not know which road to take. I stopped to consider my options. I reviewed my past. My various job experiences had all been positive, allowing me to learn about different businesses and the jobs within those businesses. My jobs exposed me to a variety of types of people and levels of employment. I learned most people do not like change. They prefer a secure, comfortable position and, for these reasons, often miss opportunities. In order to find my way, I needed to recognize opportunities and not be afraid to try something new.

Waves of opportunities constantly come towards us. If we avoid taking risks for fear of failure, the same fear blocks progress down our path. Fears come in many shapes and sizes, fear of financial failure, fear of personal failure, fear of the unknown, and fear of making the wrong decision. The best way to handle fear is to face the issue and follow our instincts.

Life is like a wave, resist and you'll be knocked over, dive in headfirst and you'll come out to the other side.
—The Best Exotic Marigold Hotel

Professional athletes are perfect examples of those who spend hours trying and failing before perfecting a move or a play. My personal advice is never quit, never stop trying, and never say something cannot be done. Continue striving and one day the perfect play will occur.

15: A curve in the road does not signify the end of the road; it all depends on how the curve is taken.

Chapter 7

The beginning of the farm

When we make correct decisions, we build confidence in ourselves. When we make a mistake, we learn. There is a lesson in every situation if we know how to extract that lesson. We cannot allow a successful decision to make us so prideful we believe we know everything, and we cannot allow an incorrect decision to demoralize us. We must be as objective as possible so next time we are better prepared and can utilize the lessons learned to guide us.

Never forget all coins always have two sides. I saw all of my jobs in the past as opportunities. In each job, I took advantage of demands or openings in the market, and when the demand ceased, I moved on to the next new market. Tired of changing jobs and learning from the ground up, I sought a more permanent solution to my long-term goals.

I needed to find a product people consume regardless of the economic environment. This was when I became interested in the food market. Milk, flour, bread, eggs, and rice are staples in any diet. Eggs seemed a good choice because the product was ready to sell without processing.

I began to formulate a business plan. I needed a customer base. This was a new challenge. In the past, I supplied goods for an existing demand. Now I had to make room in the market for an existing product. To test the market, I decided to purchase thirty dozen cartons of eggs and sell them door-to-door in my neighborhood. By making a small investment, I hoped to get a feel for the market and learn more about the egg industry.

The first decision was white or brown eggs. According to the merchant, the only difference was white eggs were cheaper. I chose the white eggs and purchased thirty dozen cartons. With the eggs loaded in my car, I set out to sell them. I was more than nervous. Selling things to your neighbors as a kid is one thing. I did not know what my neighbors would think about a twenty-year-old trying to sell them eggs. Some of the women bought the eggs without asking the price. Others compared my price to the price at the farmers market; if my price was too high they kindly bought the eggs anyway but told me next week my price needed to better.

28

It was not my intention to make a large profit, just cover my costs and build a clientele. In time, the housewives grew accustomed to me delivering their eggs once a week and began asking if I had more products to offer. My business grew steadily. I hired a friend to help me, but it still was not time for me to have my own farm. While my profits barely covered the bills, the volume sold meant I could cut out the middleman and buy directly from the wholesaler. This would increase my profit margin. I went to a local chicken farm and explained my business to the manager, a young man about my age named Victor. We negotiated a price and I began purchasing eggs at a lower cost.

16: Three things can never be taken back: the arrow shot, the spoken word, and the lost opportunity.

When my volume reached 480 dozen eggs per week, Victor offered me a reduced price. However, in order to receive the lower price, I would distribute eggs for him to his new customers. The deal seemed good, but I foresaw a future conflict of interest. Ultimately I wanted my own farm to produce and sell eggs to my own clients. I explained this to Victor and told him that before we became more involved in the business deal, I wanted to speak to the owner.

The following day Victor introduced me to the owner, a man named Mr. Oscar. I explained my plans to have my own farm. Mr. Oscar said I could continue working for him until I started my own business. He also offered to help me. I had no idea if Mr. Oscar would make good on his promise – the important thing was I had disclosed my intentions so there would be no future misunderstandings.

Mr. Oscar was true to his word. He introduced me to everyone in the industry, showed me where to buy the chicks and supplies, introduced me to the producers' association, and took me to the company that built chicken sheds. Mr. Oscar continued to help me the entire time I was in poultry farming and I am happy to say we are still friends.

I continued working for Mr. Oscar while my chicken sheds and processing plant were under construction. Once I opened the business, I spent so much time at the farm I decided to renovate the old farmhouse as a home for myself.

One of the biggest challenges I have found in creating a successful business is to define, understand, and establish a system. Without a system there is no structure and everything can quickly fall apart. Once a good system is in place, it is much easier to cope with expansion and the increase in production.

17: Providing there is demand for your product, the same amount of work goes into taking care of 100 hens as 100,000 hens, and the same amount of work goes into building five houses as building 10 houses.

Chapter 8

How I met Laura

My friend Javier called one day to ask a favor. Javier liked a girl named Andrea. Andrea would only go out with Javier provided it was a double date and Javier found a date for her friend. Javier asked if I would be the friend's date. I told him I would like to help him out but I did not like the idea of dating someone I knew nothing about. Javier said he would call me back. Five minutes later, Javier telephoned and told me the girl's name was Claudia, her age, where she studied, and where she lived. Javier was clearly desperate to go out with Andrea so I told him to count on me.

The afternoon of the date, Andrea's friend cancelled, so she convinced another friend to stand in. Javier picked me up and the first thing he said was, "Change of plans. Your date's name is Laura. Don't ask because I know nothing about her." To put this into perspective, I was doing Javier a favor and Laura was doing Andrea a favor. I did not know Andrea or Laura, and Laura only knew Andrea. We were both going out on a whim to help our friends.

What is time? Time is only the delay of what is to come.
—El Gaucho Martín Fierro

Javier and I picked up Andrea and then went to Laura's house. Javier and I waited while Andrea went to the door. Laura captured my attention the moment I saw her. She was cute with a lovely figure and a huge smile.

We went to dinner and then dancing. I have never liked dancing. I am not a good dancer; it is too much effort and the music in clubs too loud for any real conversation. Laura, however, loved to dance so

I danced a few dances and then sat and watched as Laura continued to dance. At the end of the evening, Javier and I dropped off the girls at their homes. I decided I needed to find an excuse to ask Laura out again. Two weeks later, I received an invitation to a party and decided to invite Laura.

I called and left messages but Laura did not return my phone calls. It appeared Laura wanted nothing to do with me. The more she ignored me, the more I wanted to see her, so I kept calling. When I finally got a hold of her, I asked her to go out with me that evening. Laura found a million reasons she could not go out. I found a way to get around each reason until she ran out of excuses and agreed to go out.

That evening, I told Laura about the farm and kept her laughing with my jokes. I invited her to visit the farm and bring Javier and Andrea if she liked. Laura said she would let me know.

Days passed and Laura did not call. I called her several times, but she never answered. I continued to call and, although I did not reach Laura, I had many good conversations with her mother. Although Laura did not like me, I could tell that her mother did. I considered this a good start! With support from her mother, I persisted and Laura and I began dating.

I couldn't dance but I was fun to be around and soon Laura began introducing me to her friends. I was twenty-three and ready for a more serious relationship. Laura was only eighteen and hesitant to make a serious commitment. While we continued dating, I concentrated on my business and Laura pursued her education. Four years later, the farm was bringing in enough income to support a family, the farmhouse was fully liveable, and Laura was finishing college. I decided to ask Laura to marry me. To my delight, she said yes and we began planning the wedding.

18: You know you're in love when the days spent with the one you love are far too short.

Laura's close friend, Father Carlos, agreed to officiate. We were married at Stella Maris church in Carrasco Montevideo. Our friends and family attended the wedding along with everyone in the poultry industry and the nuns Laura studied under. The party lasted all night. The next morning we left for our honeymoon in the United States.

My wife is my best friend. Without her support, I would not be where I am today. Throughout uncertain times, Laura showed me the right path to take. She is grounded in her beliefs and has infinite faith in us.

You never know what the future will bring. That's why I recommend you go out, socialize, and expose yourself to as many situations possible. You may find a solution to your problem, a new opportunity, or even love where you least expect it. If you never push yourself out the door, you risk missing opportunities. I wonder what would've happened had I decided to stay home that night.

19: Do not be afraid to take risks but be afraid of not trying.

Chapter 9

Life on the farm

Our days on the farm were happy ones. We had lambs, sheep, rabbits, dogs, cats, cows, and, of course, chickens. We also had honey bees. I kept my distance from the bees and left the beekeeping to my godfather.

On one occasion, a friend of mine came to the farm. He boasted that he was an expert beekeeper. I pointed to the hives in the distance and said, "Go ahead and take a look." He suited up and headed for the hives. A few moments later he ran back flailing his arms and trying to remove his bee suit. It was one of those times you laugh, even though you know you shouldn't.

He later admitted he had not properly closed the netting on his hat. The bees found the opening and started flying into his suit. By the time he realized his mistake, he had a suit full of bees. So much for being an expert!

20: Every man to his own trade.

Each morning Laura prepared breakfast and we ate sitting next to the fireplace. While Laura finished getting ready for her job at a school, I went outside to start our truck: it was an ancient thing we nicknamed "Alcatraz" because it should have long been out of service. Alcatraz was so old I had to start it with an iron crank handle. On cold mornings, I wore gloves to keep my hands from sticking to the metal. Once the engine started, I hopped in, revved it up until the engine warmed up and then honked the horn.

Laura would come running out of the house, hop in and off we went. The bus driver came to know us and always tipped his hat to Laura and waved to me. With Laura safely on her way, I returned to the farm and immediately checked to make sure the water dispensers had not frozen, stopping the flow of water to the sheds. If chickens do not have running water, they become stressed, and can stop laying eggs, which is the last thing a chicken farmer wants!

I had two employees, Javier and his mother, Maria. Javier worked alongside me. Maria sorted and classified the eggs. On Mondays and Thursdays, a distributor collected the eggs for delivery and left empty cases for us to refill. Once a week, we processed the chicken feed in our factory and twice a week new chicks hatched. Hatching days were particularly busy because of the complex incubation process. It was hard work; we worked steadily throughout the day, often without a break.

Laura prepared dinner each night. We ate next to the fireplace, talking about our day, and watching the sheep graze outside our window. The crackling wood and flickering flames created an otherworldly, peaceful ambiance.

In the early morning hours, I again stoked the fire to keep the house warm. We woke at dawn. From the comfort of our bed, we looked over the pastures. In winter, the sun's reflection glistened like diamonds on the frosty grass. When it came to the weather, we loved storms. The entire property would explode with crashes of lightning then the farmhouse would rattle with the roar of thunder.

Spring was lambing season, a beautiful and exciting time. From our bedroom window, we watched the lambs being born. One morning, I surprised Laura by bringing in a newborn lamb and placing it next to her while she slept. It was a rare and wonderful morning we will never forget.

We lived a simple and happy life. We worked a lot but we did not mind. Our combined incomes provided us with a comfortable life. We continued to invest in the business. We bought another truck, a used Citroen with high mileage but a good engine. Pleased with our purchase, we drove home congratulating ourselves on the deal we made and commenting how the truck ran. Then, it began to rain. The truck's roof leaked so badly that, within minutes, it was as wet inside as it was out. Soaked to the bone, we laughed the whole way home.

Around this time, we had fantastic news, Laura was pregnant. This was a special time in our lives. Laura enjoyed her career and the business was growing. We could not have asked for anything more in our lives. We had everything we wanted.

21: If you do not love, you deprive yourself of the opportunity to know maximum happiness.

Chapter 10

Everything changes

In Uruguay, at the time, individuals could not obtain credit. Personal purchases like houses and cars must be paid-in-full at the moment of the transactions. Only businesses could obtain credit. When I started the business, I used the farm as collateral to secure a loan to finance the costs of starting up. As soon as I started making a profit, I began paying off my loan.

22: Extending credit to someone with no experience is setting him up for failure.

When people get a credit card but have no experience at using it, many times they buy items they cannot afford. By the time they realize they are too far in debt, it is too late. My philosophy is: no credit is better than bad credit.

One of the first things I did was join the Uruguayan Poultry Producers Association. I was the youngest member with the smallest farm. As a member, I had contact with the industry's largest producers and access to invaluable information. The Internet did not exist in those days and it was difficult for individuals to have up-to-date and accurate information about the industry. The poultry association met monthly to discuss the direction of the market and the fluctuating price of chicken feed.

23: Information and insight into the current market is extremely valuable when determining in which direction to take your company.

At the time, chicken farming was a solid and profitable industry. Farmers with large and established farms had the luxury of setting aside capital reserves. New farmers, like me, used our profits to repay loans. Chicken farming was an industry in which everyone could prosper. At least that's what I thought.

In reality, chicken farming was cyclical, just like any other business. In a growing market, existing farmers purchased more chickens and expanded production. Others saw an opportunity and started farming. The combination of the expansion of existing businesses and new businesses entering the industry over-saturated the market, creating a glut of goods. Everyone in the industry began to suffer. Farmers with capital reserves survived. Farmers without savings and large debts struggled. The crisis forced a large number of farmers out of business.

Many of the large producers were wise country people with keen insight and knowledge about the market and life, in general. These experienced farmers had extraordinary powers of observation and an innate ability to analyze situations. I loved hearing their stories and predictions and appreciated the simplicity with which they expressed things. Through them, I learned one of the most important business lessons of my life.

As part of the poultry association's efforts to unite and fortify the industry for the tough times ahead, I had the honor to be selected to visit farmers and explain the benefits of joining the association. On one occasion, I visited the farms with one of the directors of the association. As we drove from farm to farm, he gave me three pieces of advice I have never forgotten:

**24: When it rains you have to build dams
because it does not always rain.**

25: The best time to save money is when you have money.

26: Go to the banks to save money, not to take money out.

These words still guide me today, but when I first heard them I thought, "It's easy for him to say because he has money. How do I do it with no money?" It took me a while to discover the answer. You save money slowly, step-by-step, a little at a time. When we are young, we want to reach the top as quickly as possible, skipping crucial steps along the way. The price for skipping those steps—the price for failing to implement a system—is that everything crumbles.

27: The best way to save money is to spend less than you earn.

Chapter 11

When the banks stop being your friend

Even during the height of the farming economy, the members of the poultry association anticipated change. The question was what, when and how we would be affected. The change came sooner than expected with an increase in the price of grain. Once they started, prices rose rapidly and kept rising.

Uruguay is a small country with a total population less than one third that of Los Angeles County. Changes in the global economy have an enormous impact on small economies like Uruguay's, especially when the changes affect imports or exports like corn, sorghum, grain and sunflower seed. If a country producing these products has a poor harvest, the shortage results in higher prices and greater demand. Countries with small economies have limited buying power and cannot compete with world economies.

28: It's always darkest before dawn.

Feed prices became extremely volatile. No one could predict what would happen next. Large farms had the cash reserves to buy in bulk and the lucky, or wise ones, stockpiled enough feed to last an entire year before the price increase. Small farms, like mine, lacked funds to buy in bulk and had no choice but to buy grain at market price.

It was a battle to stay afloat. Farmers who survived the first round soon faced an even more challenging second round as we battled against depreciating prices. This combination of falling egg prices and rising grain prices had a devastating effect on the smaller farmers. The larger farmers, who stockpiled grain at a lower price, fared better. If I painted a picture of the situation, it would look like this: The biggest farmers have been sitting in the stands watching the weakest farmers fight to the death with the monsters in the arena.

As hard as I tried to make the farm work, survival was impossible. These economic forces were too strong and were beyond my control. The battle weakened my resolve. Out of desperation, I sought a line of credit from my bank but the loan would not cover our costs or keep us afloat during the tough times.

I was forced to consider my options. To be honest, there were not many and none were good:

A: Request an increased line of credit on my existing loan. I doubted my bank would agree once they looked at our finances and the economic state of the poultry industry.

B: I had an offer to borrow money from a friend at no interest but I could not guarantee my ability to pay them back. This made me uncomfortable.

C: Approach other banks for loans. This was risky and increased our vulnerability.

All things considered, I decided to approach other banks for loans.

29: A banker is a fellow who lends you his umbrella when the sun is shining, but wants it back the minute it begins to rain. – Mark Twain

I went from bank to bank. No one was prepared to loan large amounts but I obtained a number of small loans. I used the first loan to repay my original loan, and the second loan to pay off the first. When I paid off a loan, I renegotiated another larger loan. Eventually, I had loans from five different banks. This was possible because the banks did not communicate with each other. They looked solely at my business not other debts. By paying off loans, either all at once or in large sums, I increased my credit limit and secured more loans.

When I ask people if they know how to negotiate, they usually admit they don't, and add that they have never negotiated. However, we negotiate every day. Each time we want something, we persuade someone to give it to us. This is negotiation. We negotiate what to do next weekend, where to go for dinner, what to watch on television, and our children's curfews. A negotiation does not need to involve money but merely persuading the other person in order to reach a mutual agreement. We are all negotiators in life. We practice negotiating every day, several times a day, but are often unaware we are negotiating.

My job now consisted of going from bank to bank, acquiring and paying off loans. I spent so much time looking for money I no longer had time to do my work at the farm. While the business suffered, none of this really helped because the high interest charges simply dug me further in debt. A similar situation occurs when people max-out their credit cards then only make the minimum payments. Before long, they owe more than they originally charged. I was sitting on a ticking time bomb, waiting for it to explode.

Each bank manager was different. Some managers were good, others abused their power. One particularly helpful manager greeted me when I came in and told his assistant to take good care of me and see that I got what I needed. He always said, "If we don't help our clients, who will? That's what the banks are for." I remember him fondly.

On the opposite end of the spectrum, one manager made me wait three hours before seeing me. I always smiled and thanked him for his time. I made sure to tell him that I appreciated how busy he was and knew his time was valuable.

I call this strategy of running from bank to bank, "the carousel" since I was going around and around, getting nowhere, and ending up back where I started.

I called borrowing from one bank to repay another "the bicycle." Pedal up meant borrowing. Pedal down signified repayment. Borrow, repay. Borrow, repay. I had to keep pedalling faster and faster just to keep the bicycle moving.

30: A bank is a place that will lend you money if you can prove that you don't need it. – Bob Hope

We continued this method of borrowing, digging ourselves a deeper hole of debt. To make matters worse, the price of eggs continued to fall. The future looked discouraging. It was essential that we maintained faith in ourselves and did not lose our enthusiasm. If we lose our enthusiasm we see the world through a negative lens, but if we maintain our enthusiasm we see the world through a positive lens and will have the strength to prevail.

Despite our failing business and ever-increasing debt, this was an exciting time in our lives. Laura's belly was beginning to show and we were both thrilled by the thought of having a baby. I tried not to worry her but Laura realized our current situation was unsustainable. Understandably, she wanted to know what we were going to do.

I had to be realistic. We could not fall further in debt waiting for the economy to improve. Time was running out. I stayed up nights trying to come up with a solution. I needed to find work outside the farming industry but where and doing what? Then I met the man in the marble and granite industry and found a risk worth taking: Leave Uruguay for the uncertainty of America.

31: If you are willing to do only what's easy, life will be hard. But if you are willing to do what's hard, life will be easy. – T. Harv Eker

Chapter 12

When we came to the United States

When we arrived in California, we did not know the difference between hotels and motels. Tired from travelling, we stopped at the first place with a vacancy sign. That night we learned the very meaning of "cheap motel". Thin walls, cars coming and going, voices in the hallways (in a language foreign to us), and doors constantly opening and closing meant we barely slept. The thing I remember most was feeling unsafe and thinking we must find a decent place to live.

The next morning, Laura and I set out to find somewhere safer and better to live. The weather was cold and cloudy. In Uruguay, damp, cold, gray mornings meant rain and cold temperatures throughout the day so we dressed appropriately. We left the motel at seven thirty in order to arrive at the first apartments by eight. In Southern California, there is a marine layer that makes mornings gray and damp. By noon, the fog burns off to reveal bright sunny skies and warm weather. We also found the rental offices closed until 10 a.m. but the worst was yet to come.

In Uruguay, people paid for everything in cash. In the United States, everyone expects you to pay by check and have a credit history. This is especially true for renters. The first apartment manager handed us a long form to complete. We stared blankly at the paper. We had no idea what a social security number was. Current address? None. Phone? No. Bank account? Not yet. Emergency contact? Laura and I simply looked at each other. We could fill in our names but nothing else.

I tried to explain we did not need to fill out paperwork because we could pay in cash. To prove this, and in case the manager did not understand I pulled a wad of bills from my pocket. Obviously this was not a good tactic. As soon as the manager saw the money, she said she was sorry. They had no vacancies.

We moved on. Some places told us to fill in as much information as possible, and they would see what they could do for us. When we explained that we had no way for them to contact us and were living in a motel, the interview usually came to an abrupt end. I should mention, practically all of this was done in sign language, because neither of us spoke English.

32: Don't worry about what you can't do and if you can do it. Do it and stop worrying about it.

Finding a place to live was beginning to seem impossible. However, neither of us ever considered giving up. Instead, we shifted our focus to finding a commercial location which we hoped might prove easier than finding an apartment. The Uruguayan company had instructed us to set up the business in Anaheim, in an area called "tile mile." We knew the location but had no idea how to go about renting a commercial unit or whom to contact for help.

The next morning we woke up to overcast, gray skies, but knew not to dress for rain. We left the motel in search of a good workspace. The first building we came to appeared vacant. We looked through the window into a vast space with offices and a reception area but no people. We heard noises coming from the back so we knocked on the door. A tall man in his mid-thirties with grey hair and glasses appeared from the back wiping the sweat from his brow. When he opened the door, I asked in my best English if he spoke any Spanish.

My heart pounded with joy when he answered in Spanish, "Of course, I'm Cuban. My name is Miguel, how can I help you?" Laura and I introduced ourselves and explained we recently arrived from Uruguay and needed a unit to rent for the twelve containers of granite tile on the way to the states. Miguel suggested we speak to one of the owners who were due to arrive from Miami in two days. Hoping the company might also be interested in purchasing some tile, we told Miguel we would return in two days.

In the meantime, we visited other businesses to check out their materials and prices. None of the businesses offered tiles similar to the ones we were importing. We could not decide whether this was a good sign or bad sign.

We went to McDonald's for lunch. That same McDonald's is still there to this day. The restaurant was full so we took our hamburgers and drinks and continued to explore the area. When we finished eating, we put our trash into the empty bag and continued walking. Ahead, I saw a man putting paper into a blue bin. I told Laura to wait while I disposed of our trash. I flattened the trash and stuffed it through the slot. We had done about all we could, so we returned to the motel and made a list of potential apartments to see.

Later we found out the blue bin was a mailbox! If anyone thinks moving to a foreign country is easy, believe me, it is not. In retrospect, many things seem funny, but they certainly weren't at the time. Each day brought new frustrations.

33: He who does not look forward stays behind or falls into the ditch in front of him.

Chapter 13

Never give up

Two days later we returned to the mile of tile to meet Sergio. It was a good day. First, Sergio was happy to speak with us in Spanish. Second, Sergio needed inventory to fill the large space he had rented. He agreed to take our granite on consignment at an agreed price. Whatever he sold, he could keep the mark-up.

34: All that glitters is not gold.

Sergio asked where we lived. We described the motel and our struggle getting an apartment. "You guys are crazy," he said, "coming here not knowing anyone or anything and with a baby on the way!"

I am not sure whether he felt sorry for us, or identified with us because he couldn't speak English himself, but he offered to help. He asked his wife, Inés, who spoke English, to call the apartment manager and say we were on our way. In the car, Sergio told us not to worry. Inés would do the talking and deal with the forms and he would co-sign the lease for us. An hour later we had the keys to our new apartment. We moved in that afternoon. The rest of the day is a blur. I do remember we got our first full night's sleep.

The next morning Sergio and Inés arrived bright and early to take us shopping for furniture and a car. On the way to the dealership, Sergio advised us to purchase the car and everything else on credit because, in the United States, you did not exist without credit. I explained we preferred to pay cash but Sergio assured us he knew what he was talking about and would help us build our credit by co-signing on the loan.

Everything was happening so fast—a little too fast—and I felt overwhelmed. We appreciated Sergio's help to establish credit and find a place to live but our priorities were different from Sergio's. Our goal was to repay our debt in Uruguay before spending more money than necessary in America. We did not want to feel pressured into buying things we might later regret. After we purchased the car, we thanked Sergio and Inés but said we would go furniture shopping on our own later.

Buying furniture taught us yet another lesson. The quantity of furniture and range of styles shocked us. Everything in the United States was on a big scale. At the furniture store, I heard one of the salesmen speaking Spanish so I asked if he could help us. We explained that we had just arrived from Uruguay and needed a bed and a kitchen table. After looking at a wide range of furniture, we chose the least expensive.

The salesman asked if we would like to open a store credit card in order to receive a special discount on our purchases. We were certainly interested in the discount. I explained we could not qualify for credit, but we were prepared to pay in full in cash, would that qualify us for the additional discount?

That day, I realized cash now took a back seat to credit. The large retail stores were not interested in offering a discount for cash because by financing the purchases, they had the opportunity to make an additional 18% to 25% in finance charges.

The salesman said he wanted to see us get the discount, assured us we would qualify for credit and said to follow him to his office. We sat across from him at his desk and he began asking us questions and filling in the credit application. We told him our names and address and then he asked for our income and banking information. Although we could not provide this information, he continued to fill in the blanks. Seeing the confused looks on our faces, the salesman explained, "Trust me, we have to fill in every space on these forms or they immediately disqualify you for lack of information. As long as you make your payments on time they never check the information." When we were still reluctant, he said, "Don't worry. In America, you are expected to have credit, and the only way to get credit is with credit."

We left the store with a new credit card and a receipt with the date of delivery without paying a dime.

Where ever we went, someone tried to sell us something we did not need. We felt like the Indians during the Spanish conquest who were pressured to trade gold for worthless objects. Everyone wanted our money in exchange for things we did not need.

In less than a week, we realized life in America revolved around consumerism, having the latest and greatest of everything, bought with easy credit. In Uruguay credit was restricted to business. In America, there were no restrictions and limitless credit.

A STORY: Two Uruguayan farmers attended an international poultry seminar in another country. One farmer was extremely wealthy, yet lived an unassuming life in the countryside. The farmers decided to go to shopping mall. When they walked in, the wealthy farmer was aghast at the amount of "things" for sale. Shaking his head, he said, "I see so many things I do not need."

Consumerism has strong roots in mass advertising and the bombardment of sales, creating false needs within us. – Enrique Rojas

Chapter 14

The United States company

Our shipment of granite tiles arrived and were delivered to Sergio's as a temporary solution. I did not want to depend on Sergio any longer than necessary. The paperwork was in place to establish the company, now we needed a location.

Laura and I started attending English language classes, which I found difficult and frustrating. I did not want to waste time learning the words for table and chair. To survive and feed my family, I needed to communicate. After three classes of learning the names of furniture, I decided to learn English on my own. I bought a pair of headphones, hooked them up to the television, and watched the movie "Jaws" over and over again while repeating the words and pairing them with the action in the scenes until I fully understood their meanings.

Throughout the day, I listened for words I recognized and their context. I asked others the meanings of words and to explain their proper context. As my vocabulary expanded, I began forming sentences. After a few months, I spoke rudimentary English and was not ashamed to communicate.

Our search for a business location continued. Miguel contacted an agent who specialized in commercial properties and arranged for him to spend a day showing me potential locations. I met the agent on the agreed morning and soon discovered the agent did not speak a word of Spanish.

At each location, the agent consulted his notebook and uttered a string of words followed by "total square foot." To me, a foot meant the part of your body at the end of your leg. I could not figure out what feet had to do with the buildings. Confused, I smiled, nodded my head and followed him inside where he again rattled off a string of words and "total square foot." The realtor continued talking as we toured the buildings, and I continued smiling and nodding. This went on for six hours.

In between locations, he talked nonstop. As the day went on, he talked faster and faster until I thought my head would explode. After the first two hours, I wished he would shut up but I did not know how to say "please be quiet" in English. I have never been so relieved than when he wanted to stop for the day. I managed to get the information on the properties suitable for our business, thanked him, and said goodbye.

When I got home Laura asked how the day had gone. I said, "I am exhausted. All I want to do is lie down and sleep." For the first time in my life, I asked for an aspirin. The next morning, my mind cleared, I looked at the information for each property to determine the best one in terms of location, space, and price. In the end, we found a good location at a great price. The next step was to furnish the offices and create a workshop.

Laura was due any day and had a huge belly but continued to work. Optimistic about the future, excited about the upcoming birth and relieved to have found a location for our business, we were extremely happy.

35: When it is dark enough, you can see the stars.
– Ralph Waldo Emerson

We built four offices, purchased good quality used office furniture and built displays and showcases from wood other businesses discarded. When we finished, we had what we considered a luxurious office.

The number of perfectly good things Americans threw away amazed me. In Uruguay, people fixed, refurbished or found new uses for old items. One day my neighbor threw out a television. I asked if it no longer worked and he said, "It works but I got a new one."

This man was a perfect example of the millions of Americans on the treadmill called consumerism as we buy for the sake of buying, replacing good with better and becoming a throwaway society. In the United States, many opportunities are overlooked. Laura and I realized if we worked smart and hard, we could get ahead. According to my friend, Dan, there are enough resources for everyone in the world. What is lacking is proper distribution of these resources.

36: Half of the people in the world are starving;
the other half is dieting to lose weight.

Chapter 15

We made it

We were almost ready to open the business, but since I didn't know how to lay floor tiles, we contacted an installer. Our tiles cost six dollars per square foot; the installation cost was fifteen dollars a square foot! We were still on a tight budget so we found an installer to lay the floor for less. This decision cost us dearly in the end.

Laura was home when her contractions started. She called me at work and I immediately rushed home and left the floor installer to work on his own. We arrived in plenty of time and everything went smoothly. Although our obstetrician did not speak Spanish, his nurse did and translated during the labor and delivery. By dawn we were the parents of a beautiful baby girl. I stayed with Laura throughout the entire birth. It was an incredible experience.

They asked if we had chosen a name. Together, we answered, Sofía. The next day I picked up the birth certificate and saw they spelled Sofía with a "ph" instead of an "f" written "Sophia." To me this read *Sopia*. I did not know how to ask them to change it so I left it and hoped our daughter would like the American spelling of her name.

A few days later, Laura and Sophia were doing well so I left the hospital to see how our floor was progressing. I arrived at our office and discovered the installer had done a horrible job and stolen a considerable amount of our materials!

37: I'm not rich enough to buy inexpensive things.

My father always warns against choosing the cheapest route because then you spend double. Aside from having to have the floor redone, everything had turned out well. We were exceedingly happy. We had a gorgeous daughter, Laura was healthy, and our business was ready to open to the public. My English was not at the level that I felt confident selling the product to clients so we hired Miguel's wife, Cindy. Cindy was the ideal person for the job: she spoke English and Spanish, had secretarial experience, and knew the stone industry.

In the mornings, I worked in the office and warehouse and, in the afternoons, I contacted potential clients and returned home early to spend time with Laura and Sophia. After dinner, I put on my headphones, and continued my English classes. I learned new words each day and began forming more complex phrases. Through hard work, things were coming together.

The colors of our marble tiles were not the most popular. Fortunately, many of our clients were installers and promoted the materials for us. We were able to create this network of clients for a number of reasons. First, the majority of the installers spoke Spanish so it was easy for me to communicate with them. Second, we offered incentives for selling our materials and third, we accommodated their schedules. Other businesses closed at five o'clock. We noticed this and decided to stay open late. Extending our hours gave us an advantage over our competitors and increased our sales. We also provided a telephone number to contact us after normal office hours.

In the beginning, I completed the orders, loaded the trucks, cleaned the warehouse, directed sales, and acquired new clients. Cindy answered the phone, managed the paperwork and accounts, and attended clients who came into our office. After Laura recovered from childbirth, she wanted to return to work, so we put a playpen and a crib in the office and she brought Sophia with her.

Our business grew and we hired someone to help in the warehouse. The days were long and exhausting, but everything was going well. We began paying off our debt in Uruguay and made sure to pay all of our other bills on time. In fact, we established such good credit we received offers for more credit cards. We accepted every card, not for the purpose of buying whatever we wanted, but to build our credit history and as a safety net, in the event we needed money in an emergency. Within a few months, we accumulated a large stack of credit cards.

We were on a tight budget. While the only income we had was my salary, frugal living allowed us to pay off our debt in Uruguay within 12 months of opening our business. Laura and I agreed if it all ended at this point, even though we had no money, we could be proud of ourselves. We had moved to the United States, learned a new language, paid off our debt in Uruguay, and successfully started a new business without losing anything or hurting anyone along the way. Working hard and taking every opportunity that came our way had paid off. Grateful for having had the opportunity not only to learn from our mistakes but also to correct them, we vowed to live within our means and never fall into debt again.

I will never forget the day we sent the last check to Uruguay to pay off our debts. The future looked bright. We could begin saving and looking for new opportunities. At least that was our plan. Life is full of surprises and doesn't always go according to plan. That same afternoon, we received a phone call from the central office advising us that they were closing all of their locations, including ours!

38: Victory belongs to the most persevering.

Chapter 16

A new bump in the road

In any moment of decision, the best thing you can do is the right thing, the next best thing is the wrong thing, and the worst thing you can do is nothing. – Theodore Roosevelt

Everything happened quickly. We did not understand the company's decision to close our office. Our branch functioned independently from the main office and we were making a profit. Nevertheless, the business ceased. We were unemployed and wondering how to pay the rents on our apartment and business. In the morning, we were financially liberated but by afternoon we were financially challenged.

39: When you are forced to make a change, you are given the opportunity to explore paths you may never have considered.

We made a list of the pros and cons of our situation.

The Cons: No work, no income, responsible for the business premises, visas expire in a year.

The Pros: Healthy and able, bilingual, debt-free, excellent credit history, experience in the stone industry, very current business startup knowledge.

40: Analyze the problem in smaller parts and seek solutions to each; in the end, the whole problem will be resolved.

We considered our options. We could either return to Uruguay or stay in the United States. We were not ready to return to Uruguay. If we stayed in the United States, how would we make a living? I knew I did not want to work for someone else and proposed we start our own business but we had no capital to start a business. Borrowing again in Uruguay meant going into debt. Neither of us wanted to go back to pedaling the debt bicycle. We didn't know where to start, but we did know what we wanted. I wanted to work. Laura wanted to work, too. We would accomplish these goals without accruing debt.

41: If you don't know what you want, at least define what it is you don't want.

42: If you earn $2,000 a day and spend $2,050 you will never have enough. However, you can have enough if you earn $100 a day and spend $80.

We pondered our options and came up with a plan. I would get a job, any job. Cleaning floors or loading trucks, it didn't matter as long as it paid the bills. It was important to us to live in the United States legally with the freedom to come and go as we pleased. This meant we needed United States citizenship. Laura would look for a teaching job at an institution willing to sponsor us for citizenship. While Laura focused on finding a job, I would take over the housekeeping. Once Laura found a job, we would live off of her salary and I would focus on starting our business.

Tomorrow is another day and you can make a fresh start. For this reason, take one day at a time and do not rest until you have done your best.

To start a business, I believe you need three things: Desire, passion, and some money. In that order. Although I am a great proponent of education, there are many successful entrepreneurs without college degrees.

A STORY: A flood warning was issued for a small town. The authorities recommended everyone evacuate. One man decided to stay. He told the authorities, "God is going to help me." The water level rose. The authorities sent a boat to the man's house to rescue him before the water got too high, but the man's response was, "God is going to help me."

The water continued to rise and the current grew stronger until the man had no option but to climb onto his roof. A rescue helicopter spotted the man and offered to him a lift to safety. Again the man responded, "God is going to help me."

Eventually, the current swept the man away and he drowned. In heaven, the man came before God and said, "I thought you were going to take care of me, but you let me down."

God looked at the man and responded, "First I sent you the authorities, then a boat, and finally a helicopter, and each time you refused my help. What more did you want me to do?"

Even in adversity there will be opportunities. It is up to you to take them. Survival in business rests with you and no one else.

43: I plan my work then work my plan. – Bob Spogli

We had a plan, now it was time to set it in motion. To reduce our expenses, we moved to a smaller apartment and sold our cars. We kept the work truck to share between us. I began looking for a job but found it difficult. The Gulf War caused the United States to head into a recession and no one was hiring at that time. As a last resort, I asked Sergio if he needed a warehouse helper, lucky for me he had an open position. The job paid minimum wage but something was better than nothing. Sergio hired me to drive the forklift, to keep the place clean, and to load orders into trucks. I did these assigned tasks as well as anything else I could help with. I was happy to do the work and grateful to Sergio and Inés for the opportunity.

44: It doesn't matter how many times you fall, what matters is how many times you pick yourself back up.

45: Failure is simply the opportunity to begin again, this time more intelligently. – Henry Ford

46: Success consists of going from failure to failure without loss of enthusiasm. – Winston Churchill

We were on such a tight budget we could not even afford a daily newspaper. Luckily, the paper was delivered to the warehouse. I arrived at work early each morning and looked through the jobs section for teaching positions. If I found one, I called Laura with the details. Laura now spoke fluent English, French and Spanish, which was an advantage because many schools sought bilingual teachers.

One principal asked Laura where else she had applied. When she told him, he said she was crazy to walk through those neighborhoods alone. A number of schools offered Laura teaching positions, but none were willing to sponsor her for citizenship. I continued working at the warehouse and Laura continued her search for a teaching position. I took Sophia to work with me when Laura had interviews. If my work made it unsafe or impractical to have Sophia in the same area, I put her in a playpen next to Inés' desk. If Sophia woke or needed something, Inés called me over the intercom.

During this time, we also took part-time jobs to earn extra money. Anaheim Stadium was across the street from Sergio's business. On game nights, I stayed late with another employee and made extra money by letting Angels' fans park in our lot.

One day I came across an ad for a teaching position near our home. I called Laura and gave her the information. She took her resume in that morning and by the afternoon they had interviewed her, offered her the job, agreed to sponsor her for citizenship, and said she could bring Sophia to work with her!

47: After every storm the sun will smile. – William R. Alger

Chapter 17

A new beginning

During the eight months I worked for Sergio, customers often asked if I knew of any fabricators. Fabricators are the people or businesses that prepare the stone slabs for installation and do the final touches, such as polishing and edging. It occurred to me that fabricating was a lucrative industry. There weren't many companies that focused on fabricating, there was a large demand, and the price of fabrication was steep, despite the economic recession.

I knew I wanted to start a business—but how? My mind returned to the film industry and I began to see parallels between the process of making a movie and the process of starting a new business.

Every movie begins with an idea and every business does, too. For that idea to take shape, the movie needs an executive producer to put the project together. I would become the executive producer of my business. Movies need directors to ensure actors deliver a good performance. I needed a general manager to ensure we delivered a good product. I knew that my business would have to be like a really low, low budget movie and that I needed to be prepared to be the producer, the cameraman and even the guy who tapes down the electrical cords. Once again, I would do whatever it took to be successful.

In order to get into the fabricating business, I needed an industrial machine to cut large slabs. I began researching these machines, how much they cost, how they functioned, how they were built and what companies produced them. I looked at countless pictures, brochures, and manuals. Industrial cutting machines were particularly expensive–far too expensive for me at the time.

After studying these machines in great detail, I told Laura that I could build one. With this in mind, we developed our next plan. I would continue my day job and, at night, build my own cutting machine. While this endeavor would take all of our savings, plus using credit cards to purchase the materials for the machine, Laura and I agreed our future was worth incurring this new debt. The desire to succeed did not drown out our common sense. We both agreed to use any additional spending money to, first, pay off our credit cards.

That was how we began the fabrication business, working a minimum wage job during the day and building the machinery at night. In retrospect, I realize that when one is intensely focused on a goal, the powers of concentration will filter out all distractions until the path ahead is visible and clearly marked.

48: If you want the fish, you have to get wet.

I had no experience in fabrication so I needed to find a person who did. One day a man came into the marble warehouse and spoke to the receptionist about fabrication. After he left, I asked the receptionist what he wanted. She said he was a fabricator looking for work. Upon hearing this, I ran out to find him but he had already gone. Then, I saw a small, old white car pulling out of the lot and realized it was him. I chased after the car and knocked on the window. When he rolled down the window, I introduced myself and said I heard he was a fabricator looking for work. He confirmed this was true and told me his name was Juan. I explained I was opening a fabrication shop and would like to see his work. Juan agreed and we arranged a meeting.

We met a few days later and I showed Juan the location I planned to use for the business. He looked at the empty shop and asked where the machinery was. I admitted we did not have any machinery–yet. Then he asked if I had a piece of marble and some tools so he could show me an example of his work. I confessed I didn't have tools either.

Juan remained silent. I could tell he was thinking. The seconds ticked away. I expected him to say he was not interested in the job. Instead, Juan said if his boss agreed to loan him tools, he would bring the tools to the shop and show me his work. Surprised and pleased by his offer, I readily agreed and then asked why he was looking for a job if he had one. Juan explained his current job was too far away to continue making the trip every day in his old car. Plus, his wife was pregnant and he preferred to work closer to home in case she needed anything.

Before he left, Juan gave me the name and telephone number of his employer and agreed to return the following Saturday. I liked Juan and the fact that he volunteered his employer's contact details before I asked. Everything he said made sense. I also appreciated his good attitude. But I had my doubts whether he would return and if he didn't, who could blame him? I had an empty shop, no tools and was starting a business I knew nothing about!

When the intensity of the concentration in the task is greater, hours seem to pass by in minutes. Flow.
– Mihaly Csikszentmihalyi

Saturday came. True to his word, Juan showed up with tools and a piece of marble. As he demonstrated a variety of finishes it became clear he knew how to work with natural stone.

Impressed by his work and his knowledge of the industry, I asked when he could start and how much he needed to make. I gave Juan my word I would pay him the wages we agreed. I explained if the business failed, the liability was mine; his risk would be finding another new job. Juan is an exceptional person, helpful and kind with a mellow and calm personality.

When I built the first cutting machine, I made the supports out of wood because I could only afford to use steel on the most crucial parts and even then I used recycled steel. I did not have a welder so I put everything together with screws and bolts. The only thing I couldn't build was the cutting motor. Of course, without a motor the Bridge Saw would be worthless. A new motor was far too expensive. My only hope was to find a used motor. Cutting motors are unique and last forever. Finding a used one in relative good shape was going to be difficult.

49: Your greatest strength is the ability to identify your greatest weaknesses.

Chapter 18

The machine

During this time in our lives, Laura and I were in an ecstatic state, a state of flow. Energized and focused, we were immersed in the pursuit of our goals. Grateful for the way things had worked out, our energy and enthusiasm fuelled our positive outlook and created a path of energy. With each step, the path opened wider, inviting us forward. The future was ours. Nothing could stop us. We knew we could overcome anything that dared get in our way. Each achievement, no matter how big or small, motivated us to push on and be the best we could be.

Despite the adversities of the past and the uncertainty of the future, we were immensely happy. We had no money, but we were happy. On one occasion, I used five different cards to pay for a tool we needed. We were near the limit on our credit cards and still needed to purchase a cutting motor.

I continued to work my day job and used every spare minute to search for a cutting motor. Perseverance paid off and I found a company in Los Angeles that specialized in making machinery. On my day off, I went to see if they had a used motor I could buy. When I arrived, I explained to the receptionist what I needed. She said the only person who could help me was Ted, the owner, and if I waited a few minutes he would be coming out of the shop.

I waited, and in a few minutes, Ted came out and introduced himself. He invited me into his office and asked what business I was in. I told him I hoped to start my own fabrication business and explained I was building my machinery from scratch due to lack of funds. Ted asked more questions about my plans and graciously offered to give me a tour of his facility.

As we walked through his facility, we made small talk. Ted asked the type of car I drove and where I had parked. I said I drove an old beige Ford pickup truck and hoped it was okay but I had parked in the lot behind their building. Ted assured me that where I parked was perfect and then asked me to excuse him for a moment while he spoke with an employee. After the tour, Ted offered to walk me out. In the parking lot, two of Ted's employees were standing next to my truck with a brand new motor. Ted pointed to the back of the truck and said, "Open it so they can put the motor in."

Mortified he had mistakenly thought I wanted to buy a new motor, I put my hands out and said, "I am sorry if I did not explain myself. There is no way I can afford a new motor. I was hoping you might have a used one at a price I could afford."

Ted looked me in the eye and said, "Let them load the motor. You and I can speak privately in my office."

After they loaded the motor, I followed Ted back inside to his office. We sat and Ted reached for a pen and piece of paper as he asked the address of my shop. He said he needed it to give to the technician he was sending out to install the motor and weld everything onto the machine.

Again, I told him, "You do not understand. I can't afford the motor, much less pay a technician to install it."

Ted replied, "Don't worry; once your shop is up and running you can pay me back. I am confident everything is going to work out. If I'm not worrying, you shouldn't worry either."

I didn't know what to say, so I thanked him a million times for having faith in me. We used that machine constantly and produced many projects. With the money these projects brought in, I was able to pay Ted back. A few years later, technology advanced and Ted and I designed the first computerized machine. We also designed a remote control to allow the technician to control the main panel without walking back and forth after every cut. Years later, we used the same machine, built of wood and bolted together, when we remodeled some of Las Vegas' biggest hotels including the Mirage, the Golden Nugget, and Treasure Island. My homemade machine cut all the slabs for these hotels.

Ted and I still keep in touch, 22 years later. I can never thank him enough for the blind faith he had in me.

50: The greatest object in the universe, says a certain philosopher, is a good man struggling with adversity; yet there is still a greater, which is the good man that comes to relieve it.
– Oliver Goldsmith

Chapter 19

The first project

The bridge saw finished, I purchased the remaining hand tools for finishing edges and shining the granite and our work tables. We opened for business and received our first job from a local marble company for kitchen countertops. Before beginning the project, I asked Juan if he knew how to do the measurements. He said he did, and we went to the site to make sure there were no errors. In the shop, we went over our measurements at least five times to make sure they were correct before we started cutting the slab.

When we finished, I asked Juan if he knew how to install. He replied with a resounding "no" and explained fabricators did the cutting, installers did the installation. I said, "Not anymore!" Clearly worried, Juan repeated he did not know how to install a kitchen. I thought for a moment and then said, "Perfect, neither do I. Tomorrow we will learn together."

51: By cutting grass one learns how to be a gardener.

The following morning, we prepared everything for the installation and carefully loaded the slabs into the truck. On our way to the job, I asked Juan how he had slept, knowing his wife was due any day now. He said he slept badly not because of his wife but worrying about how we would install the kitchen. I feigned confidence for Juan's sake and did not admit I spent the night worrying which pieces to place first and how to level the counters.

When we reached the house, we measured the slabs one more time before starting the installation. We worked with intense concentration one step at a time until the kitchen all came together.

We were so proud of our work, we radiated happiness. Our enthusiasm for the finished product was catching, and soon the client was praising our work and admiring their new kitchen.

52: Measure twice, cut once.

When I started the business, I worked 14- to 16-hour days, often seven days a week, and charged each of my credit cards to the limit. Over the years, I learned capital helps start a new business but, even with capital, you must have the dedication and willingness to work hard.

Starting and running a business is like flying a plane. First, it is essential to know the plane is safe and capable of flying. In business, this means determining if your concept can fly. Second, you must know the weight of the cargo and the amount of fuel required to take off. If the cargo is too heavy or the fuel insufficient, the plane will never take off. Similarly, if costs exceed capital, your business will not get off the ground. Third, you must determine how much fuel is required to keep the plane in the air and arrive at your destination. It is the same in business. There must be enough funding for the idea to take off and enough money in reserve to keep the business flying until the destination is reached and your business is on solid ground.

Desire and passion for what you're going to do is a key to success, because you must be willing to dedicate all your time and effort to get any idea off the ground.

53: When everything seems to be going against you, remember that the airplane takes off against the wind, not with it. – Henry Ford

Balance is part of the formula.

Our business was located in a business park. The business next door to us was a well-established stone company that had been there for years. The owner's name was Steve. When the Windows Operating System computers came out, Steve bought one.

Buying that computer was the beginning of the end for Steve. He became obsessed. He spent hours on end figuring out all the different ways to use it and, at the end of each day, he disconnected the components and took the computer home as if it were a priceless treasure. At home, he set it up again and spent the evening in front of the monitor. Eventually, Steve's wife left him and his business fell apart. As I observed this happening, I realized how easy it is to take a step off your path then lose sight of where you are going. To achieve a goal you must maintain harmony between your work and the people who surround you.

During all these years I observed how technology was enslaving us, rather than helping us have more free time to enjoy with our family and friends, or doing hobbies.

When I was young, one day I saw a man with a beeper. I thought he must be very important to have this device where people could locate him at any time of the day. My desire was to one day be important enough to carry a beeper. Well, one day I got a beeper, and I quickly became very disenchanted with it. It was constantly beeping, and I had no freedom. All I wanted was to get rid of the noisy thing.

You don't know what you have until it is gone. Money buys material things like cars, houses, gold and everything we want. We may be able to "make" more money but money can't buy more time.

54: Learn from the mistakes of others because you will not live long enough to commit all on your own. – Eleanor Roosevelt

I make a conscious effort to learn from my mistakes and from the mistakes of others. I knew a man who opened a business, and began spending the money as fast as it came in. He purchased an expensive car and wined and dined his friends at nice restaurants. What the man did not realize was that the money was not his, it was his clients' and suppliers' until he had paid his suppliers and completed the jobs he had received deposits for.

I call this type of businessman the gasoline engine because they repeat the same actions with the same result. A car engine intakes gasoline, compresses it until it explodes, then releases the exhaust. Like the engine, this type of businessman receives payment from clients (intake) and immediately uses it frivolously (compression). Having spent the money, he cannot pay his suppliers, which causes a disaster (explosion) and ends in the collapse of his business (exhaust).

One of the most common reasons I have seen a new business fail is that the owner does not know how to manage the business money. They believe all the money coming in is theirs to spend but, in reality, the amount of money an owner gets to keep is remarkably small and the rest is the blood to keep the business alive and well. The same way that I learn from others' mistakes, I learn from their successes. I observe what others around me are doing and, if they are successful, I copy them by applying their methods or ideas to my life.

55: Learn from others' successes as well as from their mistakes.

Starting a business requires hard work and dedication. Starting a business without sufficient capital requires even harder work, countless hours, and patience because it will take much longer to achieve success. But it can be done. Banks are reluctant to loan to businesses open for less than four years because they know these years are the most difficult for a business to survive. If you can make it through the first few years without help from the bank, continue what you are doing because your system works. Try not to borrow. Save as you go and become your own bank.

56: Where there is a will, there is always a way.

My best advice for starting a long-lasting, successful business without the backing of a large capital is to stay debt-free by paying for everything as you go. This will help you to build a strong and healthy business. Buy only what you need. This applies to your personal life, as well as your business. Know where you stand financially at all times. Knowing how much money you have will help reduce spending and motivate you to find new ways to increase revenue. These three-letter reminders may help:

Cash on Delivery (COD): Pay for everything at the time of purchase.
Keep Tight Control (KTC): Manage your finances with an iron fist.
No Unnecessary Things (NUT): Don't go nuts; buy only what you need.

What I'm trying to convey is that you can still start a business without all of the resources in place. If you wait for everything to be perfect, you will never start anything. Things are rarely 100% perfect. Also, by waiting too long, you risk becoming disheartened and losing enthusiasm for your project.

A STORY: There were two farmers that produced watermelons and they wanted to load them into a truck to take to the local market. One farmer started to bring them close to the back of the truck while the other farmer was in charge of loading them. The second one tried to perfectly stack the melons but it took too long. The first farmer said, "By the time you finish loading, the market will be closed. You're never going to load everything perfectly into the cargo hold because every watermelon has a different size and shape; the best way to load it, is to place everything in the truck bed and as the truck drives off everything will fall into place."

I do not recommend anyone max out their credit cards as we did. At the time, we had no other option. However, we never used credit cards without considerable thought and always made paying them off a priority. It took two years to repay our credit cards after we opened our business. We worked hard and paid as much as possible towards our credit cards. Once we were debt-free, we started saving.

I believe the people who fail with the credit card system are the ones who misuse them by purchasing items that do not generate revenue. That is simply money lost.

Credit cards are designed to make people forget they are spending money. Swiping a card does not feel like spending money. Removing the money from your wallet and handing it over creates an awareness of spending. My advice is to use cash as much as possible to make you aware of the money you are spending. If you are an impulsive person, my suggestion is to leave the cards at home so you can avoid purchasing things you will regret. Delaying the purchase gives you time to decide if you need the item enough to incur debt.

A final word: If you cannot pay off your credit in full when it is due, don't use it!

Chapter 20

Why not the credit cards

While I grew up without credit cards and thus developed the habit of paying in cash, there is scientific evidence supporting my belief that no debt is good debt. I've done a lot of reading on the subject. Art Markman, Ph.D., has a particular article I found quite interesting:

"Debit and credit cards are an important part of our economic lives. These days, it is almost a surprise to go to a store and see someone pay with cash or a check.

There are many advantages of debit and credit cards, of course. They are easy to carry. You are not limited by the specific amount of money in your pocket. There is protection for cards that are lost or stolen, while money that is lost is just gone.

Obviously, credit cards have their dangers. The most obvious of these dangers is that they typically carry high interest rates. Once a consumer goes into credit card debt, it can be hard to dig out from beneath the payments.

*There is also a lot of evidence that consumers spend more money when paying with credit cards than when they are spending cash. For example, Drazen Prelec and Duncan Simester reported studies on this topic in a 2001 issue of **Marketing Letters**. In one study, they told that randomly selected participants in the study would be offered the opportunity to purchase tickets to an actual professional basketball game that had just sold out. These tickets were highly desirable. Participants were told either that they would have to pay in cash or that they would have to pay by credit card. They were asked how much they would be willing to pay for these tickets. Those who were told they would have to pay by credit card were willing to pay over twice as much on average as those who were told that they would have to pay by cash.*

What is going on here?

There are many possible explanations for the observation that people pay more when using credit cards than when using cash.

*For example, Richard Feinberg explored the link between credit cards and spending in a 1986 article in the **Journal of Consumer Research**. He varied whether people could see credit card logos while they were making purchases or leaving restaurant tips. People left higher tips and indicated that they would be willing to spend more for products when they could see a credit card logo at the time than if they could not.*

In addition, people may pay less attention to prices when they are paying by credit card than when they are paying by cash. For example, the article by Prelec and Simester cites an unpublished study by Dilip Soman suggesting that people are less likely to remember the amount they spent on a purchase when they pay with a credit card than when they pay with cash.

This last finding relates to many observations in a variety of settings that people are better able to control their behavior when they have physical objects that help to guide their behavior than if they have to think conceptually. For example, people taking food at a buffet may have the desire to control the amount of food that they eat, but they still tend to fill their plate. Thus, they eat more overall if they are given a large plate than if they are given a small plate.

Likewise, driving behavior is affected by the type of speedometer in the car. For a while, car manufacturers were putting digital speedometers in cars. It is hard for people to judge the change in speed with a digital speedometer relative to an analog speedometer, because they have to actually think about the change in numbers.

Credit cards have this character as well. To stay within a budget using a credit card, you have to remember the prices for each of the items and then keep track of how those prices relate to your overall budget. If you have cash, then you can also limit the amount of cash that you carry as a way of limiting the amount you spend without having to remember all of the purchases you have made.

As you can see, many factors come together to make it difficult to maintain a budget when spending with credit cards. Perhaps the title of the paper by Prelec and Simester says it best: 'Always leave home without it.'"

Choosing to use plastic over cash also causes people to disregard the amount of money they spend and the prices of goods. This is especially true in casinos. Here is a portion of an article by Dr. Mark D. Griffiths, Ph.D., that validated my belief in cash-only:

"The use of 'plastic payment' is well-known by those in commerce and is now being used by the gaming industry. Commercial operators know that consumers typically spend more on credit and debit cards because it is easier (and psychologically guilt-reducing) to spend using plastic. Many forms of gambling use virtual forms of money. Whether using chips, tokens, e-cash, or smart cards, they all serve the same psychological function. They 'disguise' real money's true value. What's more, chips and tokens are often re-gambled without thought or hesitation and all the evidence seems to suggest that people gamble far more with virtual forms of money than with real cash."

Chapter 21

We are on the right path

The months flew by and, despite the economic recession, our business grew at a rapid pace. We worked long hours to keep up with the work. In the mornings, Juan and I did installations and in the afternoons, Juan prepared slabs while I worked in the office. At night I put the final touches on the slabs. The business had been open less than a year and we needed to hire another person.

We had not yet made it, but we were on the right path. I have always kept a tight control of our expenses and now that we almost were out of debt, we were even more careful with our spending.

A STORY: A farmer had three daughters. The oldest was engaged to be married. When his friend asked what he intended to serve the wedding party. The farmer answered, "I don't know."

"I have a suggestion," the friend said, "kill your cow and have a big BBQ."

The father of the bride looked at him in astonishment, "Never! That cow's milk feeds my family every day. I prefer to have six gallons of milk every day than one huge feast of meat."

Successful businesses are often called "cash cows" because they provide a steady source of income. Like the farmer and his cow, look after your business and it will provide years of dependable income. Controlling costs is one way to take care of the cow.

At work and in our personal lives, we paid for everything in full at the time of purchase. If we wanted something but did not have the money, we waited. In business, paying in full and up front made us popular with the suppliers and allowed us to negotiate better prices. We still utilize this system today.

57: You can't build a reputation on what you are going to do.
– Henry Ford

I let nothing stand in my way. When a new client asked if we could do an installation in the local mountains during the snow season, I agreed without hesitation. I would find a way to deal with complications and never turned work away. The pride I took in our work brought in new clients through referrals from satisfied customers.

The job in the mountains had an unexpected impact on my life. I am truly a dog lover, and this particular client raised Labradors. The day I saw their litter of puppies I fell instantly in love and said I would like to buy one, if the price were reasonable. On the last day of the job, the couple said if I honestly wanted a puppy, they would give me one as a gift, once the puppy was weaned and had had its vaccinations.

I couldn't wait to get home and tell Laura and Sophia the good news. The next morning I contacted the apartment manager to ask if they allowed pets. The answer was 'no'. However, because we were exceptional tenants and consistently paid our rent two and a half months in advance, the manager agreed to ask the home office to make an exception.

Paying in advance is a practice that has served me well and one I highly recommend. Whenever possible, I pay a little extra on my bills. For example, when the electric bill is due, I pay 20% to 30% more than I owe. This gives me a credit on my account. I do the same with my gas, water, telephone and any other essential monthly bill. I do not do this with nonessential items such as cable television because if money were an issue, I would cancel those services. By paying a little extra each month on necessary expenses, I accrue a sizeable credit and have the security of knowing if something were to happen, and I was unable to pay the bill, my utilities would not be turned off. It also gives me time to plan instead of reacting.

Being ahead in your monthly obligations provides a sense of confidence and people around you can feel it!

This is one way how money well-managed provides independence.

The following Sunday, I went to the office and asked what the verdict was regarding our new puppy. The manager said, "Sorry, no pets." I believe things always happen for a reason, which may not become clear until further down the road.

58: When one door closes, new ones open.

If we wanted our puppy, we had to move. The decision was easy. We would move, but where? On the way back to our apartment, I came up with a solution. We would buy a house. As soon as I got to the apartment I told Laura, "We are going to buy a house today." She raised her eyebrows and said one word, "How?" I told her we would figure that out once we found the house.

That afternoon, we started looking. At an Open House, we met Joel, a hardworking, honest realtor, in his mid-50s. We explained that we had a spotless credit score and, with savings plus credit card advances, could maybe afford a down payment of five percent, but not the Standard 20%.

Joel thought for a moment and said those terms were difficult, but not impossible. Our best bet was to find a house and then negotiate the down payment with the seller. He said to give him a week to prepare a list of potential houses.

The following Sunday, we spent the day with Joel looking at houses and I came up with the idea that perhaps we should buy a house we could divide into two homes. Laura, Sophia and I would live in one side, and we would rent the other to Juan and his family. Joel liked the concept but cautioned finding a house easy to divide was the problem. Nevertheless, he was willing to try.

59: If opportunity doesn't knock, build a door. – Milton Berle

The next week we viewed more properties and, when they did not suit our needs, Joel persevered and widened our search parameters to include five- and six-bedroom homes. Finally, we found a large, easily dividable home owned by an elderly single woman wishing to downsize and move nearer her son. Joel explained our financial situation and the lady offered to carry the balance of the down payment in a 15-year loan with interest. Juan agreed to rent half the house at the same rent he paid for his much smaller apartment. Everyone was happy. We got our puppy, Juan got a larger home and the woman sold her house. By making extra payments, we paid off our loan in eight years instead of fifteen.

60: Where everyone saw a desert, one man saw Las Vegas.

A STORY: When the church decreed priests must know how to read and write, Father Joseph, a wonderful but illiterate priest, lost his job. Joseph moved from his small town to the big city and started a business. He continued helping others and giving to the poor. Over the years, Joseph's built an economic empire and became renowned for his kind nature and acts of charity. One day a journalist who was interviewing him said, "Without knowing how to read or write you became one of the country's wealthiest men. Imagine where you would be today if you had been literate?" Joseph responded, "I would still be a priest in a small town."

**61: Every change, good or bad, opens the door to
new opportunities.**

Each person has a talent. The lucky people recognize their talent. The rest of us have to discover ours by keeping an open mind, pursuing what we enjoy and do well, and finding opportunity in every situation.

*The biggest mistake people make in life is not trying to make a
living at doing what they most enjoy. – Malcolm S. Forbes*

Chapter 22

Growing pains in the shop

After a few years, our big break came when a union company subcontracted us to do the fabrication for The Mirage hotel in Las Vegas. The contract quadrupled production and required tripling our team. Along with the Las Vegas project, we continued our normal business. I focused on sales, clients and administration. Juan supervised production.

This entire time, I used the original homemade machine and generated enough profit to repay our debts, enable my family and Juan's to invest in homes and for the business to acquire the capital reserves to invest in a new machine. Ted graciously accepted the order for the new machine and enthusiastically congratulated me on our success. As he did when he supplied our first motor, Ted told me not to worry about money; he would supply whatever we required.

Choose a job you love, and you will never have to
work a day in your life. – Confucius

It's better to have too much work and have to figure out how to accomplish it than to have no work at all. Six days a week for seven months, we kept a gruelling pace completing the hotel project and continuing to expand our customer base. We were exhausted but pleased the business was going so well. Sometimes I worked so late I ended up sleeping in the shop rather than drive all the way home just to drive back again a few hours later. I tried, but found it impossible to get home from work early. For days, I did not see Laura or Sophia. The rare evenings I made it home for dinner were incredibly special.

Cisco, our dog, greeted me at the door and Sophia ran to me with open arms begging for a piggyback ride.

Ultimately, my work schedule took its toll. Laura was unhappy and I felt out of control. I had lost the balance between personal and business. I wanted to spend more time with Laura and Sophia but the business demanded my attention. There simply were not enough hours in the day.

When you own a business, the success of the business is vital not only to you and your family but to your staff as well. It takes complete dedication of your mind, soul, and time to make the business succeed. When the demands of the business take you from your family, you are faced with a dilemma—do you let your family or your business suffer? It is not an easy situation. Each person must make their own decisions and find their own balance.

For me, the biggest price I paid as a business owner was not being able to spend more time with my daughter when she was growing up.

A business can fail from too little work; it can also fail if it has more work than it can handle. The expansion of our business created growing pains, which often occur in successful businesses when sales start to exceed capability.

During these times, you question every decision you make:

- Am I ready for this challenge?
- Am I capable of completing this challenge?
- If this doesn't work, what will I do?

When I began doubting myself, I sought advice from a friend, a successful and methodical businessman. His methods worked for him but not for me. Other friends and colleagues whom I approached were too busy with their lives to sort out my problems. I continued talking to various people. I found that explaining the problem to others forced me to think about it in different ways and, little by little, a solution emerged.

After reading copious amounts of business and management books and still not finding the answers, I decided to grab the bull by the horns and find my own solution. To avoid being defeated by the enormity of the situation, I took one step at a time. I faced multiple challenges, foremost being our inability to keep up with the increased volume. We fell behind schedule and customers complained. I could not solve our production problems because I was too busy putting out fires and for every fire I extinguished, another ignited.

When you own your business the only person who is responsible for its success or failure is you. You should never expect other people to solve your problems.

I began my day on the telephone appeasing disgruntled clients. I viewed each complaint as an opportunity to understand what we were doing wrong and maintained a positive attitude by reminding myself, "It is better to have clients who complain than no clients at all!"

A STORY: A man accepted a job to drain a small swamp. The boss handed the man a two-way radio and the keys to a pickup truck towing a row boat equipped with a generator and suction pump.

"Call me on the radio to report your progress!" The boss shouted as the man drove off. After several days and no progress report, the boss radioed the man and asked why he had not reported his progress. The man shouted into the radio, "What progress? I can't get the boat in the water because of the crocodiles!"

62: Know what you're getting into before moving forward.

Juan suggested we hire more people to speed up production. We began the task of interviewing, but it proved difficult to find hard-working people who knew the trade. We hired a person who, after two weeks, answered to everything we asked for with, "That's not my job." Others proved unreliable and some just plain lazy. The more people we hired, the worse our problems became. We needed a different solution.

Thinking is the hardest work there is, which is probably the reason why so few engage in it. —Henry Ford

The answer came to me one night at a traffic light. Exhausted and impatient to get home, I prepared to go when the light turned green. As the sixth car in line, I expected to make the light. I watched the first car go and then the second. There was a slight delay between cars to start to move before the third car crept forward. The fourth car followed closely behind the third but, just as the car in front of me started to move, the light changed. The following night, I was fifth in line behind a Mercedes sports car. When the Mercedes failed to make it through the light, I realized you could have a great car and go nowhere if too many cars were in front of you or if some cars took too long to get through the light.

The same thing was happening at the shop. Our machinery was like that Mercedes getting held up on its journey to completion. The green light represented the start of the day and the red light the end of day. Our product, like the cars, could not get through fast enough. I had to find a way to make things flow faster and more smoothly in order to get everything through the line each day. Ironically, we often find solutions we would not have found had we not encountered problems. By the time I reached home I'd come up with an idea, but working on it would wait until the next day. That night I was spending time with my family.

Laura, Sophia and Cisco greeted me at the door and, for the first time in months, I felt like I was beginning to regain control. After we put Sophia to bed, Laura surprised me with the fantastic news that we were going to have another baby! Determined to spend more time with Laura and Sophia, I fell asleep with renewed enthusiasm to implement my plan and find new ways to run the business more efficiently.

Chapter 23

From idea to action

Insanity: doing the same thing over and over again and expecting different results. – Albert Einstein

Like the cars at the traffic light, certain projects were taking too long and slowing down others. My solution was to reduce congestion in our shop in order to get more products through in less time. The first step in reducing congestion was to reduce the number of employees. I chose five people to stay, not because they were the most knowledgeable, but because they were the most responsible and conscientious. Finding people to work is the easy part. Finding people who work conscientiously is the real challenge.

I asked Juan to reduce our personnel by noon. His first reaction was without them the work would not get done. I said that with them the work was not getting done either, and asked him to trust me. While Juan reduced the staff to our five best, some of whom are still with us today; I prioritized the day's jobs, putting the easiest projects first followed by the more complicated ones.

This method sped up production and alleviated the congestion. Putting the slabs requiring the least amount of work first created a steady flow and stopped the complicated pieces from slowing down production, which meant no traffic jam. This was just the beginning. Each area required analysis to devise a system of optimal productivity. There was not one solution. Certain areas required additional machinery, others increased staffing, and some both. The last key component was redistribution of tasks to balance the flow of production. Although complicated at first, once I started making adjustments everything began to fall into place.

63: Don't be afraid to take the first step. Chances are things are not as complicated as they seem.

The new system significantly increased productivity. Jobs that previously took nearly a week could be completed in two or three days. Changing the process not only allowed us to get ahead of schedule, we also worked with less effort.

One of the most important lessons I learned during this period was the importance of having time to be proactive and not to be reactive. The definition of proactive is to create or control a situation by causing something to happen rather than responding to it after it has happened. The definition of reactive is to act in response to a situation rather than creating or controlling it.

A proactive approach means that you prepare for the future instead of reacting to the past. Reacting to crises creates a greater risk for bad outcomes. The one asset every business owner has, other than cash, is time. It takes good use of time to become a proactive leader. Once time and money are invested in a business, it makes no sense to gamble with its future.

One very important part in having time to be proactive is having control over your money. Remember, **money well-managed provides security. Security well-managed provides independence. Independence well-managed provides freedom. Freedom well-managed provides happiness.**

64: It all begins with the will to do or discover something new.

This experience taught me the importance of having a system in place; without one we were in chaos, constantly behind, paying more people and producing less work! To ensure everyone adhered to the procedures, I listed our goals on placards and posted them throughout the shop:

- Work smart, not hard
- Share knowledge with your team mates
- If you don't know, ask
- Be polite and respectful to everybody

The most efficient systems are simple and include a well-defined set of policies, procedures, and processes. To achieve synchronicity within an organization, all participants must understand how and why the process works. The key to the success of any system is for the players to have a working knowledge of their position and a conceptual knowledge of their teammates' roles. It is vital to the strength of the organization for each player to understand their position. In my role as a trainer, my goal was to teach each player his or her role in achieving our "game plan" for successfully meeting the production schedule. In order to take the business to the next level, I knew it was time to take myself off the field and be more of a coach and trainer. Whenever I thought and acted like a player, my players lost their leader. Plus, if I was on the playing field, I couldn't see the full picture. Moving to the sideline allowed me to see the players and ensure they had everything necessary to succeed.

With the new system in place we increased production with fewer personnel, met our deadlines, satisfied our current clientele, and acquired additional business. Confident in our ability to meet our deadlines, we advertised that if we did not complete a client's kitchen on time, we would install it for free. We never had to install a free kitchen. Do you know why? Because of my people. Our reputation for completing work on time spread and gained us favor with the big contractors whose businesses relied on meeting deadlines.

In Dr. Robert Cialdini's book "Influence" about the importance of brand names, Harley Davison is used as an example of how deeply fans identify with the motorcycle company: "If you can persuade your customers to tattoo your name on their chests, you'll probably never have to worry about them shifting brands." I felt we had achieved this type of brand recognition and customer loyalty in our own way. The pride my people took in producing the best product possible made our work and our company unforgettable. This was our way of advertising.

This time as the company grew I wanted our expansion to be in an organized fashion. To achieve this, I decided to hire a production manager so I could focus on working <u>on</u> the business, not *in* the business. I wanted someone with a good disposition, honest and dedicated to their work. However, the focus of the production manager would be to ensure the day-to-day workload was simple and easy.

Name the greatest of all inventors. Accident. – Mark Twain

By chance, one of our supervisors brought his wife, Olga, to the office one day, and after speaking with her for a while I knew she was the right person for this job when I asked what hours she expected to work if I have a position for her and Olga responded, "Whatever is needed to get the job done right."

Olga was concerned that her lack of knowledge of the stone industry might be a problem. I assured her that that was the easy part; I told her that if she treated the team members like her children, with patience, caring, and using dialogue to find solutions, she would be fine. This is exactly what she did and Olga is still with us today. She is viewed fondly by everyone who has ever worked with her.

65: A person who does not know how to do something but wants to learn is more valuable than the person who knows how to do it but does not want to.

With Olga handling schedules and management, and Juan in charge of clients, I focused on the fluidity of production. Then we got the greatest news, Laura was ready to deliver the baby and the next day we welcomed our son Fernando into the family. We could not have asked for more! Laura was busier than ever, taking care of two children and studying to renew her teaching credential.

Once again I began looking for ways to run the business more efficiently, reduce my time at work and spend more time at home. I concentrated on devising a system where the machinery did the bulk of the heavy work and the people focused on details and quality control. To achieve this, I began designing a computer numerical control machine or CNC. At that time, CNC machines functioned poorly in our industry. They were also expensive and required the operator to understand computer programming.

Ted and I created a user-friendly CNC machine tailored to the stone industry and found a software designer to integrate a program into our design. Per our specifications, he devised a customized, yet simple programming system my people could operate. Unlike existing programs that required a computer programmer, our system was run by the team. By building our own machine, we saved money and designed a piece of equipment tailor-made to suit our needs. Sixteen years later, the machine is still going strong and in great condition.

When we introduced the machine, everyone was worried they would lose their jobs. I explained that my goal was for the equipment to make their jobs easier, not replace them. Despite my reassurances, the resistance to learn to use the machinery persisted. This became a serious problem, and not one I had anticipated.

Arguing they could do the job better than the machine, my people proposed a competition: a full day's work, man against machine, to determine which was more productive. The first two hours, the people worked like crazy and gained the advantage. As the day progressed, fatigue set in and human production decreased while the machines continued at a constant speed and rhythm; for that reason, the machines won but I wanted a win-win situation. To convince my people that automating heavy tasks benefited everyone, I proposed an entire day of automating the heavy work and letting the people attend to finishing and quality control. At the end of the day, we attained greater production and produced an improved product.

Once my people realized increasing the use of equipment made their jobs easier and relieved them of strenuous manual labor, they quickly adapted and began mass-producing with less effort. Today, almost all of the same people are still part of our team. Not surprisingly, whenever one of the machines breaks down, it seems like the end of the world and everyone realizes how much they rely on the machinery. With the shop largely mechanized, we offered clients the ability to specify template placement to accentuate areas of the slab. This gave our clients perfect and truly custom kitchen countertops.

With Olga managing the fabrication and the new program in place, I focused on developing ideas, building relationships with new clients, and spending more time with my family.

I have seen people start a business, work long hours, sacrifice time with their family, and earn less money than when they worked as an employee. The reason they found themselves working harder and earning less was because they did not delegate the work.

If you do not delegate, you become your own boss and employee at the same time. This will bottleneck your future and prevent your company from growing. Delegation is like a sport, the more you practice the better you get.

Never forget: **Money well-managed provides security. Security well-managed provides independence. Independence well-managed provides freedom. Freedom well-managed provides happiness.** These were the reasons you started your own business—to be happy, to have more time for you and your family, to have more money and to create a future of your own.

You will never "find" time for anything. If you want time you must make it. – Charles Buxton

Chapter 24

Another league

A STORY: For years I had a person who worked with me who always did his work, but when I asked him if his work was done he would answer, "Why do you always ask if I have done my work. If I had not done my work, I would have told you."

My sense of responsibility to my clients was the reason I repeatedly questioned him, but I realized that this person was the 1 out of 100 people who consistently did their job without having to be asked twice or questioned. When you find people like this the best thing you can do is surround yourself with them, and your business will run smoothly and efficiently.

The art of leadership is knowing when to drop the baton,
not disturb the orchestra.

We started to gain a reputation for being one of the best shops in the industry. We delivered a high-quality product on time, in perfect condition. If we made a mistake, we fixed it immediately to the client's satisfaction. Everything worked in harmony, but until we utilized our resources to the fullest there was room for improvement. My job was not to simply maximize production, it was to optimize production. The distinction between maximizing and optimizing is crucial to the long-term success of a business. To me, *optimizing production* means looking for the best in quality and production, while *maximizing production* focuses on looking for the most output without concern for quality.

One day a new client came in who was building a big house and wanted granite throughout. His name was Bob and when he asked for a tour of our facility I proudly offered to take him, myself. As we walked through the shop, Bob focused intently on our operation, asked numerous questions about the fabrication process and, at the end, suggested ways we might make production more efficient.

The only thing constant in life is change. – de la Rouchefoucauld

Bob's suggestions made sense and we implemented them the following day. A week later he returned to discuss his project and I showed him the changes. Impressed we acted on his advice, Bob commented that many companies fail because they refuse to adapt to an ever-changing world. I asked if he had any other suggestions for us and he said, "Stop operating like a small shop and begin operating like a factory."

I discovered Bob was a retired engineer and a consultant specializing in helping businesses produce high-quality products and minimizing production cost. Bob became our consultant but refused to accept even a dime for his services; he said he did it for personal pleasure. From Bob I learned that managing a business is like conducting an orchestra, you must listen to each instrument to discover if anyone is off the beat, and then listen to the orchestra as a whole.

A few observation and much reasoning lead to error; many observations and a little reasoning lead to truth. – Alexis Carrel

Bob loved teaching through storytelling. He told of a company so focused on production they could not see the big picture. The company made so many errors they had a separate section to repair the mistakes. They hired Bob to reduce the number of mistakes and asked him to start by assessing the mistake repair area. His advice was simple: shut it down and concentrate on not making the mistakes in the first place.

Another story Bob told was about a client who was forming a partnership and wanted Bob to ensure the potential partner did not take advantage during the negotiations. Bob advised his client not to enter a partnership with someone they did not trust. This made total sense. Why start a project with negativity? It is better not to do it at all.

Bob provided indispensable advice and helped our company move forward. He encouraged me to continue to observe and look for the parts of the process to improve. We became good friends and whenever I have a doubt, I call him for advice. He never gives me a direct answer but, instead, guides me in the right direction and allows me to develop my own solution. Bob's quotes and advice still guide me on a daily basis. My relationship with Bob is an example of the importance of listening to others. You never know who you're speaking to or how they can influence your life and future.

In a new business, the scope for improvement is large, and small changes make big differences. As the business is fine-tuned, the scope for improvement lessens and changes make less of an impact. This is where we found ourselves. After implementing a few changes that resulted in a loss of productivity, we learned to recognize when something worked, and not to mess with it!

66: If it ain't broke, don't fix it.

I also learned the importance of thorough planning before implementing changes. Quick fixes lead to chaos and cause greater loss of time and money. For me, the best method is to exercise patience by stopping to think then analyze solutions before acting. It is critical to be analytical, not to change for the sake of making change, and remember the wrong change may break something that already works.

67: We must first define the process and then control the flow by not running backwards.

I spent my first few years in business reacting, putting out fires and dealing with situations as they arose. With everything running smoothly, I had the luxury of being proactive and the time to analyze individual parts of the company to determine how they fit into and affected the overall picture.

This allowed me to turn to business books as I sought answers but, of all the books I read, only one or two had any direct application. These books were based on simple common sense, so I decided to use my own common sense.

It may be because I am dyslexic, but my ideas often stem from imagined scenarios. For example, imagine four people living in a house with a dining table that seats 10. They sit down for breakfast taking any seat they wish, place their newspapers, books or other items where they want, stay as long as they like and, when they get up, leave items scattered on the table.

Now imagine the same four people living in the same house with a dining table that seats two. Suddenly, a plan unfolds, individuals begin to communicate, meals are scheduled to enable everyone to get to work on time, and each person clears the table for the next.

I applied this scenario to our business and came to the conclusion that work space needs to complement the machinery and number of people. Too much space invited excess and encouraged disorganization, whereas smaller work spaces demanded order, fostered organization and encouraged productivity.

68: Bigger space does not mean more production.

Don't confuse size with volume. Too often people mistakenly equate the physical size of a company with production and worth, when in fact a company that occupies less space may be capable of higher production levels. Once we created more efficient work spaces better suited to our needs, we experienced greater fluidity and order to the production.

According to Wikipedia Business, Just in time (JIT) is "...a production strategy that strives to improve a business' return on investment by reducing in-process inventory and associated carrying costs. To meet JIT objectives, the process relies on signals or Kanban between different points, which are involved in the process, which tell production when to make the next part. Kanban are usually 'tickets' but can be simple visual signals, such as the presence or absence of a part on a shelf. Implemented correctly, JIT focuses on continuous improvement and can improve a manufacturing organization's return on investment, quality, and efficiency. To achieve continuous improvement key areas of focus could be flow, employee involvement and quality."

Chapter 25

Taking a break from routine

Although the business was doing well, I remained obsessed with finding ways to improve production. Ideas filled my head day and night. I tried distracting myself with television and exercise, to no avail. I felt that my business was becoming my life when I really wanted my business to be only *part* of my life.

Time spent with my family was the only thing that made me forget about the shop. Sophia and Fernando captured my full attention and exhausted me with their energy. Spending time with my family was great, but I also yearned to find something for myself, a hobby.

Through the years, I never lost my desire to fly and wondered if the United States aviation rules prohibited color-blind people from flying. After doing some research, I discovered that in the United States a color-blind person can obtain a pilot's license by passing certain tests to demonstrate visual ability to operate aircraft without endangering public safety. Excited by this, I began studying and, once I got my license, flew every day for three or four hours. Flying proved an excellent distraction and helped me return to work energized and rejuvenated.

69: Take a break from your routine; when you return you will see things from a new perspective.

Often, things become clearer from an outside perspective. To achieve this, one must find a place to discover their inner self. It's important to find somewhere tranquil to reflect, think, and grow as a being. For some, that place is a sport, or in nature, in a ministry or even in the shower. The activity can be anywhere or anything, as long as it permits reflection. I find this place when I clean. Cleaning, for me, is a mindless motion that frees my mind to ponder a problem or analyze situations over and over again.

With renewed interest in finding ways to improve the system, I gathered the team together and asked them for ideas on how we could make the shop run better and more efficiently.

After discussing our options, we decided to vote on the best idea. For their leadership and forward-thinking, I gave a reward to the person who developed a new way of working but I also rewarded every person who displayed organizational citizenship and always worked towards company goals.

Remember, trust is always a two-way street.

I trust each member of our team 100%. I would rather trust people. If that trust is abused, I'll deal with the problem at the time. Living under a cloud of doubt only serves to make life miserable while trust creates a healthy environment. Conversely, doubt creates a negative work environment.

I trust my team members to know what items they require to do their work. Every team member is issued petty cash to purchase the items they need for the job. They make these decisions independently and take pride in finding the best deals.

This is just one example of how trusting people gives them a sense of responsibility and confidence, and is a win-win situation.

Always strive to see the job through the eyes of the "team members." Be sure to recognize and reward positive attitudes and actions. This will create financial incentives that tend to drive the desired behaviors.

I refuse to waste time on pointless meetings. I communicate throughout the day with Olga for updates but only schedule meetings if someone has a new idea to propose or an issue that relates to everyone.

Part of my new management system included giving my people greater freedom to manage their own environment. I met with the fabricators and told them their job description now included developing better methods of production, training new team members, and ensuring everyone cooperated. I told them to work smart, not hard, and to achieve the best results with the least physical effort.

Entrusting people with greater responsibility is a concept I believe in. However, I was soon to learn the lesson that imposing the wrong kind of responsibility can be daunting—even to strong and productive people.

A STORY: Jackie was an accomplished hair stylist who decided to open her own salon. Six months later, Jackie closed the doors because instead of being a stylist, she spent most of her time running the business, paying bills, answering phones, managing people, dealing with subcontractors, filling out purchase orders and checking inventory.

Moral: Being a good hair stylist does not make someone a good businessperson or manager.

To be successful, business people must learn to delegate. The reason people open a business is to do better, not only financially, but in their personal lives, as well. Remember: **Money well-managed provides security. Security well-managed provides independence. Independence well-managed provides freedom. Freedom well-managed provides happiness.**

A fortunate person is one that has the time to do what they love and enjoy.

70: Develop the skills at which you are good.

A STORY: A child excelled at math, but struggled to learn Spanish. His mother, thinking she was helping, enrolled him in a language-tutoring program, and insisted he spend extra time studying Spanish. In the end, the child remained mediocre in both Spanish and mathematics, instead of developing his natural talent for math and becoming a great mathematician.

71: People rise to the highest position of their individual competency.

No one is good at everything. By recognizing our limitations and focusing on our strengths, we struggle less and become the best we can be. I applied this theory to my situation at work. I had tried to make skilled fabricators into managers, instead of letting them continue to excel at what they did best. The people I promoted were critical to the success of our team. It was crucial that I find a way to return them to their previous positions without making them feel they had failed when, in reality, I was the one who failed.

In order to have good supervisors, I first had to clarify what I expected from them and the purpose they would serve in the shop. Olga possessed the leadership qualities of a supervisor. Finding more people like Olga was not an easy task. To find what I needed, I first had to define what I was looking for. I found various definitions of a supervisor and settled on this one:

72: A supervisor's purpose is to ensure other people's jobs are simple, easy, efficient and safe.

I envisioned a leader and a rope. When the leader pulled the rope it followed. When the leader pushed the rope it bunched up and went nowhere.

The supervisor is a key element. A team's morale, performance, and quality of work depend strongly on the supervisor's character. The supervisor also plays a crucial role in the development of good attitudes.

A supervisor needs to be knowledgeable about the products but, more importantly, he or she must listen to everyone and focus on being positive. Because even supervisors make mistakes, a good supervisor must be able to admit mistakes and apologize for errors. Only then will he or she be able to help the team and facilitate an efficient work environment.

In order to produce a quality product, the supervisor first needs to understand how the team defines quality. Once the supervisor understands this, the team can begin to have a discussion about the common definition of quality.

Paraphrasing Wikipedia, quality of a product or service refers to the perception of the degree to which the product or service meets the customers' expectations. Quality has no specific meaning unless it is related to a specific function and/or object. Quality is a perceptual, conditional and somewhat subjective attribute.

Chapter 26

Why do errors happen?

73: Mistakes are caused by an accumulation of small errors.

Many of the lessons learned in one situation can be applied to another. For example, when studying for my pilot's license, I learned most aviation accidents resulted from a succession of mistakes that lead to one big mistake or accident. Despite learning this, I committed the exact series of errors myself.

One day, on a whim, I decided to fly to Las Vegas with Laura and her friend, who was visiting from Uruguay. The only aircraft available was a plane whose landing lights did not work. We planned to arrive in Las Vegas during daylight, so I did not consider the lack of landing lights a problem and decided to use it for our trip. (Error #1)

I took off from Orange County Airport. Halfway to Las Vegas we decided to land at a local airport for something to eat. (Error #2)

Back in the air, I was losing the light. I knew I-15 went straight to Las Vegas. I also knew the road followed a low elevation so I would not crash into the hills. Also, in case of an emergency, highways are one of the best places to land. I decided to use the road as visual guide instead of flying off the instruments. Unfortunately, the road I was following was not I-15! (Error #3)

When I realized we were off course, I radioed air control to confirm my location. Air control identified my position and instructed me to switch my transponder to squawk code 7700, which was alarming. Channel 7700 is reserved for planes in a state of emergency. I switched channels and the controller advised me I was flying in restricted military airspace.

Knowing that Laura and her friend had no idea channel 7700 was an emergency channel, I remained calm. Silently I recalled the definition of restricted airspace: "Areas of unusual, often invisible, hazards to aircraft such as artillery firing, aerial gunnery, or guided missiles. Penetration of restricted areas without authorization from the using or controlling agency may be extremely hazardous to the aircraft and its occupants."

I pretended nothing was wrong as I followed the controller's instructions to divert us out of the restricted zone. Once we were safely out of danger, I requested guidance to a nearby airport for landing. By this time, daylight had faded and, to complicate matters, the landing strip was under construction. After two unsuccessful approaches, I managed to land the plane safely. We eventually arrived in Las Vegas but the situation, caused by a series of errors, could have ended much worse.

My Las Vegas flight underlined the lesson that small mistakes and seemingly minor oversights can lead to big problems. I applied this theory to the shop and realized most of the problems we experienced resulted from one small mistake being passed to the next person who, unaware of the error, continued the job passing it on until the cumulative impact became a big problem.

A STORY: One day the installers returned a piece of stone to the shop and said it was not right. I gathered the team around the stone and asked them to tell me what was wrong with it. When no one could find anything wrong, I reviewed each step of the process. I said, "The estimator measured meticulously, the cutter cut precisely, the laminator ensured the veins were perfect, the polishers brought out an exceptional shine in the stone, the finishers' work was excellent and the installers installed it perfectly. This is an excellent example of the hard work of each and every person put to create a flawlessly-fabricated piece of stone. There is one problem: This is not the piece of stone the client selected. Each of you, at every stage, had the work order but no one stopped to make sure the stone matched the paperwork."

This entire time the piece remained in my hands. Next, I asked everyone to tell me the monetary value of the stone. After guessing various amounts, they looked to me for the answer. I held the stone in front of me and said, "This is the real value," as I dropped it to the floor, shattering the stone into tiny pieces. "Nothing. The stone is worthless and so is your hard work. The stone is worthless because no one checked the paperwork, assuming the previous sector had not made an error." I finished by saying the mistake was mine alone, because I had not taken the time to explain the importance for each sector to thoroughly check the paperwork.

74: The best lessons are learned from mistakes.

I continued to experiment with ways to improve production, failing along the way but always learning. I want my people to work hard and not be afraid of trying new things. If something does not turn out correctly or an oversight occurs, my people know they can admit the error without fear of retribution, and that the team will work together to rectify the situation as quickly as possible.

Once a salesman made a large error and I asked him to come to my office to talk to me. The salesman walked in and said, "You're going to fire me, right?"

"Are you crazy?" I said. "You just cost us a lot of money! What I want to know is did you learn anything?"

The salesman said he would never make that mistake again and I believed him. I told him I was not firing him because it made no sense to pay someone new to make the same mistake again.

75: A mistake admitted causes much less damage than a mistake hidden.

I trust the people I work with 100%. For example, I want the machines to be oiled twice weekly and regularly ask the manager in charge if this has been done. If he has not oiled the machines, he is honest and tells me. His sincerity is priceless to me. I gain immense satisfaction from knowing I have a team of honest people who do not fear telling the truth.

76: A company is a group of people coming together to achieve a common goal.

The above definition made me think about our company as a team with individuals in specific positions essential to the overall functioning of the team. One night, the evening news ran a feature on a basketball team whose training consisted of practicing in small groups. I wondered if creating mini self-sufficient teams would work for us. I envisioned that individuals who showed leadership ability would become team leaders and report to Olga. Apprentices who worked hard and demonstrated leadership ability would be promoted to group leaders of new groups.

This change transformed our shop from one large group into small groups of two to three, with team leaders reporting to a supervisor. This reduced the amount of time Olga spent trying to communicate with everyone and enabled her to focus on other things. Dividing the shop into independent sections prevented small mistakes from becoming big problems. Each team must check the work of the team before them in order to detect a problem early on. If an error was found, they corrected it before passing it on and compounding the mistake. Each sector was like a compartment in a large ship. If one compartment takes on water, the captain can isolate the leak and prevent the ship from sinking. This system improved operations and reduced errors, but even the best systems are not perfect.

In my opinion, one of the largest problems within almost all organizations is communication. Messages need to be precise and to the point. One rule of aviation is messages transmitted between air traffic control and the airplane pilot must be repeated back to ensure understanding. This same rule applies in business. When you explain something to an individual, ask them to repeat your instructions back to you. If the information they repeat is not the message you intended, there is a problem either with the way you transmitted the information or the way the person received it. In either case, you need to adjust your approach.

Communication must be utilized to establish a common ground and to understand everyone's perspective in order to avoid a misunderstanding.

One day I attended a screening with a friend of mine, a movie director. After the screening, a number of people approached and congratulated her on the film but they especially appreciated the way she expressed certain situations in the film and how closely they related to these situations. After everybody left, she turned to me and said, "People always congratulate me for how I expressed certain feelings and emotions throughout the film. The funny thing is that the emotions they perceive are not the emotions I was trying to express. In fact, my intentions are usually quite different."

I realized that even in a film, every person sees and understands situations from their point-of-view and that each person's point-of-view depends on their present state of being, age, social status, and education. It is important to remember that, in order for communication to be effective, you must have some background about the person with whom you are communicating. Defining terms also improves communication; for example, in our shop we use an "X" on a template to signify that the edges need to be finished and an "O" to signify that it needs to be polished. Everyone on our team knows what this means, therefore there are no problems understanding what the "X" and "O" means.

These are my guidelines for effective communication: Be specific when you talk; share your thoughts out loud with the other person; speak simply and clearly. When you have finished, ask the listener to repeat back what you said. Lastly, communication is not just about talking. Good communicators know how to listen.

77: Effective communication is an art that is necessary for success.

Chapter 27

The experts

The new systems improved our organization, but we still lacked an efficient method of measuring productivity and cost.

One day, when filling my car with gas, the concept of measuring a product in accurate terms suddenly hit me. At a gas station you don't ask for two pounds of gas because the price of gas is measured in terms of gallons. In our shop, we spoke about production in terms of slabs or kitchens but on the sales side of the business we calculated product and fabrication costs in square feet. We needed to standardize our measuring system.

Square feet became our standard of measurement throughout our business. The challenge was to establish a way to measure individual productivity and labor. A few years earlier, I had attended a contracting course taught by a supposed expert on measuring productivity and quantifying costs. I hired this expert to devise a formula for our business to measure cost of production.

My long-time consultant, Bob, questioned the wisdom of bringing in an analyst. I told Bob I would let him know the outcome.

The analyst set up a computer at the office to input, quantify and analyze data. He spent two weeks observing our operation and then developed forms for my people to complete each day. The forms required them to log a large amount of information, including number of hours worked, slabs cut, square inches per slab, etc. My first thought was that these forms would be time-consuming and burdensome. Further, they involved too much information for my people to remember. I suspected the forms would be a distraction and decrease productivity. However, this guy was the expert, so I assumed he knew what he was doing. Most of us make the same mistake of assuming experts are always right and, despite our own experiences and intuitions, we follow what they prescribe.

78: You have to know the oxen with which you plow.

I waited to see how this new process developed. Day after day, my people filled in the forms. My expert sat behind stacks of paperwork inputting data. After a few weeks, I asked to see the results. He said they were not ready. I asked other questions and received wordy responses filled with technical terms and references to comparisons and extrapolations. This continued until I became so frustrated I told the analyst for simple and concrete answers, not a lot of technical gibberish. This had no effect. I continued to get convoluted answers. My next approach was to ask for an accounting of the analysis and how the data was being compiled. John responded in yet another complex and confusing answer completely void of concrete information. This is when I learned:

79: If someone explains something in a complicated manner it's because they either don't want you to know what they are talking about or they don't know what they are talking about.

One day the analyst came to me confused as to why one of my team members achieved high productivity on some days and virtually no productivity on other days. I spoke with this person and he confessed he did not know how to write. He did not want to let the analyst down so he filled in the forms to the best of his ability. I thanked the team member for his honesty and suspected he was not alone in his struggle to complete the forms.

I realized this desire to analyze production and labor costs was imposing unnecessary stress on my people. Suddenly the image of stacks of forms sitting on the analyst's desk flashed through my mind. I imagined someone filling up a trash can with trash, and being surprised that when they emptied it, the only thing that came out was trash! The analyst was costing me a lot of money, driving my people crazy and not producing any concrete results.

After I walked with my team member back into the shop, I told Olga to collect all of the forms. I met with the analyst and cancelled the program. After he left my office, I called Bob to tell him he was right. I had made a huge mistake but I had also learned not to interrupt the workflow in my quest for improvement.

I realize an "expert" sometimes is a person who tells us what we already know, and even charges for it. Follow your instincts; if it has four legs, wags its tail, and barks, it's usually a dog.

Anyone who has never made a mistake has never tried anything new. – Albert Einstein

My next idea was to have software developed to analyze production so we could measure and improve it. To achieve this, I hired a computer programmer and invested considerable time and money. When the software was finally finished, it was useless! When we entered data into the program, our entire computer system froze. Another failure and another lesson, but at least I knew two methods that did not work.

Remember when I said you have to expose yourself to new things and if you fail you must continue to search. I say this from experience.

80: The comfort of success stifles creativity but failure forces us to learn and try new things.

Chapter 28

Listen and help

81: What goes around comes around.

The entrance to our business features a gallery of photos of Laura and me with various celebrities. After seeing the photos, a new client told me he recognized me but could not remember from where. I said I definitely remembered him. He was the real estate agent who found the first building for us. Now that I could hold a conversation in English, I invited him in to my office and we talked.

He asked how I met the people in the photographs so I told him the story of a Saturday evening years ago. I had worked late and was just going to turn off the lights when a man came in and asked if we could do a job for him. I explained we were closed on the weekends but someone would be happy to help him first thing Monday morning. The man insisted he must find someone to complete his project and do it on time. The man was clearly desperate, so I continued to listen. After he described the project and his deadlines, I explained that the complexity of the job would make it difficult to complete within his time frame. Hearing this, his face turned red and he shouted that he didn't care how difficult the job was, he needed it done by the deadline and did not care what it cost! Seeing his distress, I decided to look at the project and see what I could do to help.

82: When you help others, you help yourself because whatever you give comes back in greater quantity.

I took the job and made it a priority. By working additional hours, we completed the project ahead of the deadline. The client was so grateful and happy with the work that he insisted on finding a way to thank me. He asked if I liked music and when I answered yes, he said he would arrange VIP tickets to the American Music Awards with backstage access and passes for the rehearsals. I doubted anything would come of it but accepted his offer and thanked him. He wrote down my name as it appeared on my identification, the full name of the person I intended to bring, and told me the dates and location of the theatre. As he left, he reminded me I would need to show my identification at the gate.

Before raising Laura's hopes, I wanted to make sure the offer was for real so I went alone to the first day of rehearsals at the Shrine Auditorium in Los Angeles. To my surprise, I was on a special guest list and treated like a VIP with full access, including backstage! The next day when I took Laura to the rehearsals we ran into our client who spent the afternoon introducing us to people in the show business industry, some of whom ended up being good friends.

Laura and I, and even our children, have attended numerous award shows, walked on many red carpets and met people in the entertainment business. Who would have thought my decision to help a customer would lead to such a benefit?

Good things come when we least expect them, and from unexpected sources. Taking the time to listen and doing what we can to help others without expectation of receiving anything in return opens up unlimited possibilities. We never know who we might meet or down which path destiny will lead us.

After the real estate agent heard my story, he said, "When we first met, you spoke no English and didn't have a penny to your name. Now look at you! What's your secret?"

"It's no secret," I explained. "Work hard and work honest. Treat everyone fairly, be kind, just, and sincere. Never be afraid to try or to fail and, when you fail, try again."

Chapter 29

The search continues to find the right method

Life is like riding a bicycle. To keep your balance, you must keep moving.
— Albert Einstein

After my failures with the analyst and software programmer, Bob told me to stop running around like a chicken with its head cut off, not knowing where I came from or where I was going. He advised me to make a plan and then plot the path to move forward. As is often the case, the answer came in an unexpected form. Sophia had just turned 16, gotten her driver's license, and enrolled in a driver safety course. The course curriculum included regaining control of an out-of-control vehicle, awareness of road dangers, and analyzing information while driving to predict and avoid accidents. I decided to accompany Sophia to these classes. The topic of the first lecture was "The Three A's." We walked into the class and, written in large letters across the board, was:

Attention
Anticipation
Action

The principle of "the three A's" of good driving included paying *Attention* to everything happening on the road at all times, in order to *Anticipate* what will occur next, making time to take *Action* to prevent or avoid it.

I considered how to apply the same principle to improve operations. First, I paid attention to the dynamics and logistics of the shop. I realized over the years, without intending to, I had lost my close connection with the people in the shop.

One of my firm beliefs is that a place of work should always appear clean and tidy not only for the clients but for the people working in that environment. To regain the intimacy, I took a hands-on approach as I cleaned the shop, scrubbed bathrooms and assisted wherever I could. As a business owner you must be open to do what is necessary at any time, and never think you are above certain jobs.

Then I started using the machinery and cutting slabs. Working closely with my people reminded me that my job was to serve them and to help meet their needs. With this new realization, new opportunities arose.

A STORY: A shoe manufacturer sent two salesmen to discover new markets in the Australian desert. The first salesman's report said, "No opportunities. Indigenous people do not wear shoes." The second salesman's report said, "Vast opportunities! Indigenous people have not worn shoes – until now!"

83: Where one person sees obstacles, another sees opportunities.

I have never underestimated the value of the people I work with or attempted to create a hierarchy of power. I believe we are all equal, regardless of title. For example, Olga, Juan and I have never had a designated parking spot. Our parking lot is first come, first serve. If I arrive late in the day, the only parking spot available may be across the street and that is where I will park. The only parking rule we have ever had is to always leave two spaces in front for our clients. After all, they pay the bills.

Equality within an organization does not mean each person performs the same. I wanted to establish positions and create levels of compensation that would keep people happy and motivate them to continually improve our operations. To do this, I looked for ways of redistributing income to compensate people based on their ability to achieve better quality and greater production. I focused on developing a method of providing incentives, based on quality and production.

In Uruguay, large companies outsource parts of their business to third parties called *Fasoneros*. For example, poultry Fasoneros raise chicks to maturity for wholesalers. The Fasonero is paid based on the weight of the mature chickens. Therefore, it is in his best interest to raise plump chickens.

I liked this method and decided to make some sections of our shop Fasoneros. Each section of the shop would be like a small business run by the people under the umbrella of the company. The Fasonero concept worked because it encouraged each person to maximize their talents for a common goal.

84: All my failures pay off.

Under this system, the atmosphere in the shop changed radically when my employees realized they had the power to achieve change on their own. Team members began coordinating efforts to find the most effective way to produce high-quality products under deadlines. It was a win-win situation for everyone. Previously, I tried to control everything; now each department controls themselves, everyone is happy and more productive, and I have more time to focus on other things. I had finally found a way of letting my people manage themselves in a way that gave them the opportunity to earn more and achieve greater satisfaction at work.

Business owners tend to pay workers as little as possible in order to maximize profits. I believe a better way to maximize profits is to focus on maximizing job satisfaction and personal gratification. The key to accomplishing this goal is to establish a strong system of teamwork, where each player is equally committed and shares in the success of the team.

A STORY: A Pig and a Chicken are walking down the road. The Chicken says, "Hey, Pig, I was thinking we should open a restaurant!" Pig replies, "Hmmm, maybe, what would we call it?" The Chicken responds, "How about 'Ham-N-Eggs?'" The Pig thinks for a moment and says, "No, thanks. I'd be committed but you'd only be involved!"

Empowering my teams in this way was a big change, and change, by its nature, creates turbulence. However, I was confident that, like water, our company would level out again, hopefully at a higher level.

85: Water always seeks its own level.

During these years I invested heavily in machinery. Eventually our machines performed the majority of the heavy work and the teams completed the finer work and focused on quality. I searched for a definition of quality to communicate my ideals. This is what I settled on:

86: Quality can be measured by how proud you are of your work.

One thing began to happen. Our business grew again because clients appreciated our quality and told other people.

Expanding the concept further, we developed a system in which the production controlled itself. We eliminated regular work hours and each team determined their own schedule. I trusted my people to produce high-quality work by the deadline and did not care what hours they chose to work or if they were five minutes or two hours late. In our company, each individual completes and signs their time sheet. It is a system of autonomy and mutual trust.

Autonomy in business respects individuals by putting them in control of their work to give them a greater sense of responsibility, achievement, and job satisfaction.

In our company we offer interest-free company loans to team members who require money for personal needs. There is no set schedule of repayment. The team member repays the loan in the amount they can, as they can.

We also give our team members salary advances. If a team member consistently asks for a salary advance this alerts me to the fact that he or she may not be making enough to cover their expenses, and it is the time to review their salary.

I define a comfortable life as making enough income to pay for your monthly expenses, and still have extra to put aside for a rainy day, because **money well-managed provides security. Security well-managed provides independence. Independence well-managed provides freedom. Freedom well-managed provides happiness.**

People talked about us, and our name became renowned. Whenever I met someone from the industry and told them the name of the company where I work, they always had something positive to say.

87: It's very important to be applauded when you go on stage, but it is more important to be missed once you exit the stage.

When I started the business, I knew the only race we ran was against ourselves. That's why I had to ensure every day was better than the previous day. Instead of worrying about our competitors, I focused on how we were doing and how we could improve.

Barking, Sancho, is a signal we are riding. – Don Quixote

A STORY: Don Quixote and his squire, Sancho Panza, were riding their horses on a very dark night when they heard the sound of dogs barking. The dogs were barking at the sound of the horses and this signalled to Don Quixote that they were moving.

Each time I heard people speaking of our company I felt like Don Quixote and Sancho Panza riding in the darkness of night. Our actions were causing a reaction. You never hear about people who don't take risks or do nothing, you hear about the people who are doing something. We were being talked about, which was good, but it would have been a mistake to think we could stop improving.

There is always room for improvement and I am constantly looking for new ways to do things and setting new goals for myself and business. Once a business achieves a certain level of success, finding ways to improve becomes more difficult. This is where I found myself. I was afraid of breaking something that already worked. I don't like utilizing outdated systems, on the other hand, if something works, I don't change it. Why waste time reinventing the wheel?

A clip on TED about teaching and creativity called "Ideas Worth Spreading," by Sir Ken Robinson, highlighted the fact that wristwatches, once very popular and worn by nearly everyone, are becoming obsolete amongst the newer generations. Whereas the wristwatch used to be the only mobile method of telling time, today there are alternatives, such as the cell phone, which are multifunctional.

Some years ago, the computer industry predicted a new generation would grow with the technology. They were right. To my parents' generation, people born pre-1945, computers were strange and new. Computers became more commonplace for the Baby Boomers, familiar to the Buster generation, standard fare for the Millennials, and taken for granted by Generation Z, the digital generation born in this age of instant access and apps.

Modern technology creates a rapidly-changing world. This is why I believe it is crucial to stay abreast of what is happening in your industry and in the world at large, in order to make up-to-date and informed business decisions.

88: When I look around and see that everything is going well, it's because I'm not looking close enough.

Chapter 30

Define the method

The future of the company lay solely on me; no one else was going to do this job. In my search for ways to improve our business, I consulted my sister, who is a psychologist. She suggested I investigate a method of analysis created by Albert Humphrey. This is how I learned about a powerful and simple tool called SWOT, a model for determining the strengths, weaknesses, opportunities and threats of a situation. Using the SWOT system I developed new business and production techniques.

The concept of SWOT begins with identifying the strength and weakness of your personality or business and the advantages and disadvantages of your situation using the following guidelines:

Strengths:
Characteristics that are advantageous.

←——————————

Weaknesses:
Characteristics that create disadvantages.

Opportunities:
Elements that can be capitalized upon.

←——————————

Threats:
Elements likely to create trouble or prohibit progress.

89: Strength brings opportunities and weakness brings threats.

As the person who made the major decisions and chose the direction the company took, success or failure rested on my shoulders. My choices would reflect my personality, but what was my personality? Knowing myself was the key and the first step of strategizing the best course for the company. Using the SWOT model, I analyzed my strengths and weaknesses then used my strengths to further develop and move the business forward. I also sought out people who would compensate for my weaknesses in the context of the SWOT model, specifically aspects of the business I do not enjoy or positions I am not particularly good at. This does not include positions such as accountants, lawyers, insurance agents and other specialized areas that should be handled by professionals you trust. It is impossible for a business owner to know all the laws or be an expert in all fields. If you try to fill these specialized positions yourself to save money, in the long run it will cost you a fortune.

To begin my SWOT analysis I took out a sheet of paper and made two headings, strengths and weaknesses. I considered the things I did well, my natural abilities, and the jobs I disliked, or struggled with. I also took into consideration genetic weaknesses:

Strengths
Goal-oriented with the ability to get things done.
Open to change. Not afraid of a challenge.
Possess mechanical and engineering skills with ability to build things.
Dyslexia creates natural ability to visualize concepts.
Impatient optimist (I am impatient but I always believe things can be done).

Weaknesses
Dyslexia makes writing difficult.
Color-blindness limits my ability to choose colors.
Tendency to be too focused and consumed by work.
Frustrated by anything that is a waste of time.
Impatient and rushes into projects. Wants things done immediately.
Not a methodical person.

90: Strengthen your strengths and let someone replace you in areas of weakness.

I considered how my personality traits affected my thoughts and behavior. I imagined my personality as a pliable ball of clay taking shape as I added information. I could not yet visualize the end product, but a clearer understanding of my self began to emerge. I discovered I was not a methodical person. To balance my weakness, I needed a methodical person on my team.

The SWOT method helped create a team of complementary personalities that strengthened our company. It is not enough to know your own strengths and weaknesses you must know those of your team members to enable you to know whom to help or whom to ask for help, depending on the situation.

91: Goals that have no deadline can easily become just ideas.

My strengths include getting things done quickly. My weaknesses included impatience so I focused on short-term goals. By capitalizing on my strengths, I was able to turn threats (long-term goals) into opportunities (short-term goals). The better I knew myself, the more I understood why I enjoyed the things I did. Being impatient, I like short-term goals because they give me an immediate sense of accomplishment and gratification.

A STORY: Jack stood at the bottom of the stairs and wanted to be at the top but from his position the top looked very far away. Lacking super powers, Jack could not achieve his goal in a single bound so he decided to take it step-by-step. The number of steps did not matter because Jack was only concerned with one step at a time. Before he knew it, Jack reached the top without ever feeling overwhelmed by the task.

Each of Jack's steps represented an accomplishment. I like short-term goals because, if I fall, it is easier to recover. I can assess and prepare for the worst thing that could happen in my attempt to reach the next step; and if the worst does not happen, all the better!

92: Step-by-step you can get very far.

I like to observe nature and mimic certain behaviors that occur in our natural world. Rams provide an excellent example of how preparation strengthens action. Prior to attacking, a ram takes a couple steps back to give him greater force. But he is not stupid; a ram does not run into a wall or something he cannot conquer. The flying formation of geese is an excellent example of the benefits of teamwork. When a goose falls out of formation it immediately feels the drag and resistance of flying alone and quickly moves back into line to take advantage of the lifting power of the birds in front.

When you want to achieve a certain goal you must continue trying until you reach the right approach. A big part of the future is created by the actions we do today. By considering our actions, we can often guess the future. For example, if a car travels at high velocity towards a concrete wall, we can all imagine that car's future before the collision occurs. The future is a reflection of the actions of the present. We cannot control 100% of the future but a big part of it will be the result of the actions we take in the present.

Knowing the strengths and weaknesses of each person in the team is essential. Asking someone to do something they are not capable of is senseless. As leaders, if we expect someone to do a job they are not prepared for, the fault is ours if they fail. It is like expecting your dog to talk. Dogs are great companions and serve many purposes, but we cannot make them speak.

Similarly, trying to teach a person to swim who lacks the interest, curiosity, or desire to learn is a waste of time and you may both end up drowning.

93: Dogs can't talk.

It is not always possible to know someone's strengths and weaknesses, which is why we have a rule in the shop that if anyone is assigned a task they are uncomfortable with, they can speak up without fear of repercussion. No one is obligated to do a task if they don't feel comfortable.

My office door is always open. Members of my team know they are welcome to come to me directly without passing through a secretary or receptionist.

Clients are important but team members are even more important because without happy team members I can never have happy customers.

I make a point to regularly walk through the shop giving people the opportunity to talk to me in their own environment instead of coming to my office.

It is essential to distribute the work and define each team member's role. In my opinion, smart owners, supervisors and managers realize they are not always right and, for this reason, remain open to suggestions from team members. Once I flew to San Francisco with a pilot friend. Prior to taking off, we did not designate a pilot or co-pilot, or define our individual responsibilities. During the flight, I noticed we were flying lower than what we were supposed to and I asked my friend why. He said he thought I was in charge of the altitude. Fortunately we had time to correct our mistake. This is a perfect example of what happens when you do not communicate. We were both trained pilots with many hours of flying experience, yet failure to establish our responsibilities inadvertently put us in danger. Aviation taught me that whether you are the pilot or the co-pilot, if you see a problem you immediately report it and never be intimidated by position or seniority. Everyone's life aboard the plane is at stake and it is not a matter of rank any more, it's a matter of life or death.

Flying also taught me the importance of making a list of steps to check while performing routine activities. A simple list can eliminate distractions and shortcuts that often lead to errors.

94: If you allow an exception to the law, the exception becomes the new norm, then the new rule and, eventually, the new law.

To maintain order within a business, exceptions should not be made to company policies and procedures. Allowing one person to break a rule sets an example that others can do the same, and soon the rule becomes irrelevant. The exception becomes the new standard and the new standard becomes the new rule.

The core rules in our company are cast in stone because they serve to create a high standard of etiquette and mutual respect. These rules include practicing basic, good manners, such as greeting and helping one another.

Chapter 31

Right before the 2008 economic crisis

In 2008, Sophia was studying psychology at college and Fernando had applied to a unique arts school that combined the standard curriculum with an arts education. Although gaining admission was difficult, it was something Fernando wanted very much, so he focused on his grades and completed extra projects to help him get in. Both of our kids loved what they were doing. Now that they were older and gaining independence, Laura had more free time on her hands.

During these years housing prices increased weekly. Existing homeowners considered themselves winners while those who had not invested in a house felt like losers. One thing many homeowners failed to realize was if they had a mortgage they did not actually own their home. Most mortgages require the house as collateral. "Homeowners" are allowed to reside in the houses on the condition payments are made as agreed.

I felt the economy was out of control. People were purchasing homes and then spending additional money on new carpets, flooring, kitchens and bathrooms which, fortunately for us, often included granite countertops. Money seemed to fall from trees for these people. They spent their disposable income on new cars, new televisions, new computers, and travel. No one noticed that wages failed to rise at the same rate as house prices or the price of goods. There was a time when 100 dollars seemed like a lot of money. Suddenly it rarely covered the cost of a trip to the grocery store. Rent prices rose with house prices. No one seem to notice the economic signs, they just kept spending and borrowing.

95: If you are in debt, somebody owns a part of you.

Television advertisements encouraged people to buy and to finance these purchases. Finance companies jumped on the bandwagon and encouraged people to take advantage of increased house prices by acquiring extra cash through equity loans on homes already heavily financed.

People spent money they did not have on items they did not need thanks to the availability of easy credit. Millions of Americans seemed oblivious to the economic risks they were taking, and did not realize this type of spending was unsustainable. It's basic math, spend more than you earn and the result will be a negative balance with no resources to reverse it. Over the years, we met financially successful people in a variety of industries, including the entertainment industry. Unfortunately, we have seen many lose their fortunes because they failed to save or invest any of the money they made.

96: Never spend money you don't have on items you don't need to impress people you don't know.

One of my clients, an extremely generous but financially short-sighted man, spent money like there was no tomorrow. He hired private jets to take groups of people from Los Angeles to New York, put them up in penthouse suites and bought tickets for the best seats to Broadway shows. He spent thousands on these weekend getaways. When the 2008 financial crisis hit, this man lost everything. With hindsight, he says he learned his lesson and promises once he starts making money again to save and invest instead of throwing it all away.

Businesses and the market are dynamic and constantly changing. A good idea that proved successful at one point may later be obsolete. Ever-changing market trends demand we continuously learn and adapt.

Chapter 32

Life's lessons put to the test

It is not the strongest of the species that survives,
nor the most intelligent that survives. It is the one that is the
most adaptable to change. — *Attributed to Charles Darwin*

When things change rapidly, it is imperative to react as quickly as possible by analyzing the facts and promptly reaching a conclusion. Often the decision you make will be based on instinct. The greater your knowledge and understanding of your business, the better equipped you will be to quickly make decisions and confidently rely on your instinct.

During the housing boom, our business thrived and I practiced the same philosophy I have always had: when you earn, you save. When the financial reality changed, people did not believe they could go from such abundance to facing an economic crisis. By the time they finally noticed they were sitting on a ticking time bomb, it was too late; all they could do was to wait.

When the economic crisis hit Uruguay, our young business did not have the reserves to survive, so we decided to move to the United States and start over. We now faced a similar economic crisis in America. Fortunately, our situation this time was different. Although we faced new challenges, I realized how the large, established Uruguayan farmers had felt when the industry collapsed around them.

97: Any problem that can be solved with money is not a problem, as long as you have the money to do it: it's an expense.

Fabricating stone for large construction companies made up the majority our business. These same construction companies now faced an economic crisis. I envisioned the companies as a fully-loaded train speeding out of control. To save themselves from crashing, the engineer must slow the train. His only options are to slam on the brakes hard or reduce the load.

The large builders were deeply committed to massive building projects where they had purchased the land and, in many cases, started construction of new homes. With hundreds of homes under construction the builders faced a drastically-reduced market. Abandoning the projects at this stage was not a viable alternative, so they took the next available step of significantly reducing the cost of goods. This had an enormous effect on our business. Although our costs remained the same, we paid the same amount of rent, utilities etc., we were now faced with supplying the product for a lot less money. The price of a product may be determined by the market, but the quality of that product is determined by the people who make it. I never let quality suffer because of the reduced price.

Just when I thought our company was on stable ground, I was forced to reinvent the wheel, reorganize everything and do it immediately. Every aspect of production, the work, prices, and travel distances of the projects required reassessing, and everything in the system redesigned. My first concern was how to reorganize my business and adapt to these new conditions without distressing my team members. Ironically, weeks before I struggled to find ways to improve the system because it ran so well, now I was challenged with how to keep it afloat.

I realized how fragile stability is and how quickly things can change from one minute to the next. Fortunately, I anticipated something like this would happen and tried to be prepared for it. The fact that we had no debt made it easier for us to adjust to the ever-changing business climate. Since Laura had much more free time on her hands, I asked her to come in and help at the office.

Reacting and making changes can happen quickly in small companies. In larger companies, the reaction time increases because change takes longer and is more difficult to implement. It's like comparing a cat to an elephant. The cat is small, quick, and agile. The elephant, on the other hand, is large, heavy, and slow to move.

The decline in the economy hit us in two ways. We suffered from lower prices and a reduction in volume. Our system was designed to handle high and constant volume. Suddenly the flow of work became erratic, dwindling, drying up, surging and then dwindling again. This went on for about one and a half to two years.

The flow of production was like a water pipe with air in it. For periods, the flow is continuous and then water mixes with air and spurts out in stops and starts, splashing everywhere.

I felt like the captain of a ship in a hurricane as I struggled to keep ship and crew safe until the seas calmed. Luckily, I had the best ship, the newest technology, and best crew available. I watched other ships in the same situation go adrift and struggle to stay afloat each time a wave hit. I kept reminding myself every situation is an opportunity to learn something new. Experiencing and surviving the economic downturn definitely reassured me of that.

I am fascinated that people who become physically handicapped immediately seek ways to overcome the handicap or develop alternative talents. Yet, when the handicap is an economic one, people waste valuable time doing nothing, hoping it will fix itself. For me, doing nothing has never been an option. Challenging times call for focus and well-thought-out decisions.

In these economic rough seas I needed to zero in on the best course of action, not be distracted by too many options, and focus on the basics. This was the moment I prepared for by paying a little bit extra on my bills and paying for everything cash on delivery and never succumbing to the temptation of accepting credit. Now I just had to follow my intuition. This was the moment of truth. I would learn if my self-imposed rules, philosophies and theories would stand the test or be debunked. Everything I had done to this point was for a reason. I reviewed the things I had strived for and accomplished:

- Build a solid company that provides security for my family and my team.
- Create a work environment where people belong and feel comfortable, happy, and glad to be working.
- In all matters, treat everyone with respect.
- Allow people the independence to be self-sufficient and to work with minimal interference.
- Create a team mentality within the company where each person understands that by helping each other they help themselves.

- Establish a business that encourages and fosters creativity.
- Allow people to make the day-to-day decisions that affect their jobs and their lives.
- Allow people the opportunity to achieve whatever they want to achieve and to take pride in their achievements.

When you lose, don't lose the lesson. – *Dalai Lama*

I began to see large companies that had not prepared for the new economic realities begin to fail. When under pressure there's no time to analyze every option nor is there the luxury of making haphazard decisions. In these situations, balancing knowledge and intuition is essential. I recalled signs they used to post by the train tracks that read: Stop, Listen, Look, and Continue. It made common sense to consult your senses before acting, so I applied it to my situation:

- I stopped and focused solely on the things that affected us directly.
- I listened by consulting my team members for advice on the best direction to take.
- I looked around to see what was occurring in other businesses, then determined how it affected my business both positively and negatively.

Judge your success by what you had to give up in order to get it.
– Dalai Lama

My senses checked, I continued devising a plan. Of all the books I have read, one proverb has always stayed with me:

98: Readers of books have an advantage over the ignorant.
Over those are the ones who remember what they have read.

Over those, are the ones who understand what they have read. Over those, are the ones who put it into practice.

It was time to put the teachings into practice. First, I gathered my people to discuss how the economic situation affected us. I explained that much less work would be coming in and we would be charging a significantly lower price for our labor. To get through this crisis we were all going to have to take a share of the burden. I reassured them I would not lower their wages, but explained less work meant fewer hours worked, which would cause a decrease in their incomes.

I did not have to explain that the entire country was in economic crisis; it was all over the news, everyone knew it was a reality. I told my people I understood if they needed to look for work elsewhere and assured them the door would be open when they wished to return. Some people decided to return to their home countries for the time being. Others said they would stay with me until the end. Our company slowly shrank and eventually we were left with our All-Star players. We reorganized the groups and my people began defining their new functions the way they believed it would work best.

My people were doing an excellent job readjusting and managing fabrication, so I dedicated myself to finding more work. My goal was to ensure our prices remained competitive and the customers were satisfied so that my people made enough money to survive. To keep our suppliers happy, I continued to pay cash on delivery for our orders.

I cannot repeat how strongly I believe that anyone who starts a business is well-advised to pay for everything at the time of delivery and to resist taking out loans. This method of payment eliminates all worry about paying bills and frees you to focus on improving your business. Taking out loans and delaying payment by using credit cards is like falling into a spider web. If you don't manage it well, you'll be trapped in no time. I'm not saying never to use credit, but I am advocating you use it very wisely.

99: It's better to have money and not need it, than to not have money when you need it.

Between 2010 and 2011 we produced a great amount of work with very few people, and became more organized and efficient than any time in our past. It was incredible. Two or three days after taking measurements for a job, my people had the product ready for installation. Our clients were pleased and by the beginning of 2012 we had so much work coming in we added more machinery. When new construction companies started contacting us for work, I believed we had made it through the storm. Here is my personal summary:

- Always do what is morally correct.
- Never leave for tomorrow what you can do today.
- Always make dams when it rains because you never know when it will rain again.
- Always pay a little bit more than you owe on your monthly bills.
- Don't be afraid of failure, be afraid of not trying.
- Always be modest and helpful with the people you work with, your customers, and everyone around you.
- Always tell the truth, say what you're thinking and most importantly share your feelings and your point-of-view. Never lie in order to get your way.

Experience is that wonderful thing that enables you to recognize a mistake when you make it again. – Franklin P. Jones

And, in fact, you can find the lack of basic resources, material resources, contributes to unhappiness, but the increase in material resources do not increase happiness. – Mihaly Csikszentmihalyi

When prosperity comes, don't use all of it. – *Confucius*

We live in a society that measures the success of the individual based on the amount of material possessions he has and, under these parameters, we can never be happy because we will never have enough. There will always be a new car model, a faster computer, a bigger TV, a faster phone or someone who has more than us. This is why I consider the purpose of money is to achieve financial independence and not material slavery. If we seek money just to uphold an image and to impress people who don't matter to us, we will continue consuming things we don't need, paying bills we can't afford, and collecting junk in our garages. The purpose of money is to give us independence, and through our conscious actions and purchasing habits, we are the only ones who can achieve this goal.

A STORY: There was once a man who grew roses in his backyard to sell. He took great pride and care in his roses. One day one of his customers came to him and said, "You grow wonderful roses, why don't you utilize more of your garden space to grow more roses?"

The man stopped to think for a moment and then asked, "Why should I grow more roses?"

The customer replied, "To make more money, buy the land next to you, grow even more roses and make more money."

The man asked again, "For what?"

The customer replied, "To buy more land and grow more roses."

The man asked again, "For what?"

The customer replied, "To become a huge company and have so much money and free time, so you can sit back, and relax and take the time to enjoy the beauty and smell of your flowers."

The man paused for a moment and replied, "I already do that."

The old thinkers. Epicurus, Seneca and even the Aymara put it this way, a poor person is not someone who has little but one who needs infinitely more, and more and more. – José Mujica, President of Uruguay

Do not say, "I can't," even as a joke because the unconscious has no sense of humor; it takes it seriously, and reminds you every time. – Facundo Cabral.

And, finally, I leave you with these inspirations:

If you have a wish and your wish is to have your own business, go for it.

It is never too late to start if it is what you really want.

Always try new things and don't be scared.

When opportunities come, you don't let them go to waste.

We can produce more wealth, but we cannot produce more time, so enjoy every minute of every day.

I hope you can have a great journey like I do.

Always find a new opportunity during change.

Please always follow your dreams; it will be an incredible road.

Never stop trying.

Gabriel

Memoir

This book was written from notes I have taken and my personal experiences. I wrote this book so I would not forget the steps I took to reach where I am today, and in hopes these lessons might serve you as well as they have served me.

Sayings

1: Happiness is not something ready made. It comes from your own actions. – Dalai Lama

2: A picture is worth a thousand words.

3: Strike while the iron is hot.

4: Quality is pride of workmanship.

5: I will see how deep the river is once I start to cross it.

6: You can't get something for nothing. If it sounds too good to be true, it probably is.

7: He who has nothing to lose has everything to gain.

8: The secret to receiving the desired answer is in formulating the right question.

9: Let your work speak to your character even when you're not around.

10: Persevere and you will triumph.

11: Where a captain rules, a sailor has no sway.

12: Don't bite off more than you can chew.

13: Water under the bridge.

14: Every cloud has a silver lining.

15: A curve in the road does not signify the end of the road; it all depends on how the curve is taken.

16: Three things can never be taken back: the arrow shot, the spoken word, and the lost opportunity.

17: Providing there is demand for your product, the same amount of work goes into taking care of 100 hens as 100,000 hens, and the same amount of work goes into building five houses as building 10 houses.

18: You know you're in love when the days spent with her are far too short.

19: Do not be afraid to take risks but be afraid of not trying.

20: Every man to his own trade.

21: If you do not love, you deprive yourself of the opportunity to know maximum happiness.

22: Extending credit to someone with no experience is setting him up for failure.

23: Information and insight into the current market is extremely valuable when determining which direction to take your company.

24: When it rains you have to build dams because it does not always rain.

25: The best time to save money is when you have money.

26: Go to the banks to save money, not to take money out.

27: The best way to save money is to spend less than you earn.

28: It's always darkest before dawn.

29: A banker is a fellow who lends you his umbrella when the sun is shining, but wants it back the minute it begins to rain. – Mark Twain

30: A bank is a place that will lend you money if you can prove that you don't need it. – Bob Hope

31: If you are willing to do only what's easy, life will be hard. But if you are willing to do what's hard, life will be easy. – T. Harv Eker

32: Don't worry about what you can't do, and if you can do it. Do it and stop worrying about it.

33: He who does not look forward stays behind or falls into the ditch in front of him.

34: All that glitters is not gold.

35: When it is dark enough, you can see the stars. – Ralph Waldo Emerson

36: Half of the people in the world are starving, the other half are dieting to lose weight.

37: I'm not rich enough to buy inexpensive things.

38: Victory belongs to the most persevering.

39: When you are forced to make a change, you are given the opportunity to explore paths you may never have considered.

40: Analyze the problem in smaller parts and seek solutions to each; in the end the whole problem will be resolved.

41: If you don't know what you want, at least define what it is you don't want.

42: If you earn $2,000 a day and spend $2,050 you will never have enough. However, you can have enough if you earn $100 a day and spend $80.

43: I plan my work then work my plan. – Bob Spogli

44: It doesn't matter how many times you fall, what matters is how many times you pick yourself back up.

45: Failure is simply the opportunity to begin again, this time more intelligently. – Henry Ford

46: Success consists of going from failure to failure without loss of enthusiasm. – Winston Churchill

47: After every storm the sun will smile. – William R. Alger

48: If you want the fish, you have to get wet.

49: Your greatest strength is the ability to identify your greatest weaknesses.

50: The greatest object in the universe, says a certain philosopher, is a good man struggling with adversity; yet there is still a greater, which is the good man that comes to relieve it. – Oliver Goldsmith

51: By cutting grass one learns how to be a gardener.

52: Measure twice, cut once.

53: When everything seems to be going against you, remember that the airplane   takes off against the wind, not with it. – Henry Ford

54: Learn from the mistakes of others because you will not live long enough to commit all on your own. – Eleanor Roosevelt

55: Learn from others' successes as well as from their mistakes.

56: Where there is a will, there is always a way.

57: You can't build a reputation on what you are going to do. – Henry Ford

58: When one door closes, new ones open.

59: If opportunity doesn't knock, build a door. – Milton Berle

60: Where everyone saw a desert, one man saw Las Vegas.

61: Every change, good or bad, opens the door to new opportunities.

62: Know what you're getting into before moving forward.

63: Don't be afraid to take the first step. Chances are things are not as complicated as they seem.

64: It all begins with the will to do or discover something new.

65: A person who does not know how to do something but wants to learn is more valuable than the person who knows how to do it but does not want to.

66: If it ain't broke, don't fix it.

67: We must first define the process and then control the flow by not running backwards.

68: Bigger space does not mean more production.

69: Take a break from your routine, when you return you will see things from a new perspective.

70: Develop the skills at which you are good.

71: People rise to the highest position of their individual competency.

72: A supervisor's purpose is to ensure other people's jobs are simple, easy, efficient and safe.

73: Mistakes are caused by an accumulation of small errors.

74: The best lessons are learned from mistakes.

75: A mistake admitted causes much less damage than a mistake hidden.

76: A company is a group of people coming together to achieve a common goal.

77: Effective communication is an art that is necessary for success.

78: You have to know the oxen with which you plow.

79: If someone explains something in a complicated manner it's because they either don't want you to know what they are talking about or they don't know what they are talking about.

80: The comfort of success stifles creativity but failure forces us to learn and try new things.

81: What goes around comes around.

82: When you help others, you help yourself because whatever you give comes back in greater quantity.

83: Where one person sees obstacles, another sees opportunities.

84: All my failures pay off.

85: Water always seeks its own level.

86: Quality can be measured by how proud you are of your work.

87: It's very important to be applauded when you go on stage but it is more important to be missed once you exit the stage.

88: When I look around and see that everything is going well, it's because I'm not looking close enough.

89: Strength brings opportunities and weakness brings threats.

90: Strengthen your strengths and let someone replace you in areas of weakness.

91: Goals that have no deadline can easily become just ideas.

92: Step-by-step you can get very far.

93: Dogs can't talk.

94: If you allow an exception to the law, the exception becomes the new norm, then the new rule and eventually the new law.

95: If you are in debt, somebody owns a part of you.

96: Never spend money you don't have on items you don't need to impress people you don't know.

97: Any problem that can be solved with money is not a problem as long as you have the money to do it: it's an expense.

98: Readers of books have an advantage over the ignorant.
Over those, are the ones who remember what they have read.
Over those, are the ones who understand what they have read.
Over those, are the ones who put it to practice.

99: It's better to have money and not need it, than to not have money when you need it.
Saying # 100 is on you:
100: ....?

Quotes that have formed my way of business

For everyone who asks, receives. Everyone who seeks will find. And to everyone who knocks, the door will be opened.

A man's mistakes are his portals of discovery. – James Joyce

Life is like a wave, resist and you'll be knocked over, dive in headfirst and you'll come out the other side. – The Best Exotic Marigold Hotel

What is Time? Time is only the delay of what is to come. – El Gaucho Martín Fierro

Consumerism has strong roots in mass advertising and the bombardment of sales, creating false needs within us. – Enrique Rojas

The biggest mistake people make is not making a living at doing what they most enjoy. – Malcolm S. Forbes

Choose a job you love, and you will never have to work a day in your life. –Confucius

Thinking is the hardest work there is, which is probably the reason why so few engage in it. – Henry Ford

Insanity: doing the same thing over and over again and expecting different results. – Albert Einstein

You will never "find" time for anything. If you want time you must make it. –Charles Buxton

The art of leadership is knowing when to drop the baton, not disturb the orchestra.

The only thing constant in life is change. – de la Rouchefoucauld

Anyone who has never made a mistake has never tried anything new. – Albert Einstein

Life is like riding a bicycle. To keep your balance, you must keep moving. –Albert Einstein

Barking, Sancho, is a signal we are riding. – Don Quixote

Experience is that wonderful thing that enables you to recognize a mistake when you make it again. – Franklin P. Jones

And, in fact, you can find the lack of basic resources, material resources, contributes to unhappiness, but the increase in material resources do not increase happiness. – Mihaly Csikszentmihalyi

When prosperity comes, don't use all of it. – Confucius

The old thinkers. Epicurus, Seneca and even the Aymara put it this way, a poor person is not someone who has little but one who needs infinitely more, and more, and more. This is a cultural issue. – Jose Mujica, President of Uruguay

Well done, Gabriel!

How wonderful that you have put your story onto paper!
I am certain the book will entertain and inspire many, and be considered a treasure by your children, their children, and generations to come!

Melissa